D1094545

MUNICH

Blunder, Plot, or Tragic Necessity?

PROBLEMS IN EUROPEAN CIVILIZATION

MUNICH

Blunder, Plot, or Tragic Necessity?

EDITED WITH AN INTRODUCTION BY

Dwight E. Lee

CLARK UNIVERSITY

D. C. HEATH AND COMPANY
A Division of Raytheon Education Company
Lexington, Massachusetts

Library of Congress Number: 72–83696

CONTENTS

INTRODUCTION

MUNICH has apparently become firmly fixed in our vocabulary as a symbol of shameful surrender to the bullying tactics of an aggressor. It has, indeed, been misused to justify intransigence in international conflicts when a parallel with the Munich situation hardly existed. How to account for Munich is a question that arose almost before the ink was dry on the Agreement of September 29, 1938. But before turning to that problem we must take a look at a related phenomenon, "appeasement," which has incurred the opprobrium associated with Munich.

The Munich Agreement represented the apogee of the appeasement policy which Great Britain had followed from the early 1920's and France from 1936. It was a popular and defensible policy as pursued by British governments from about 1920 to the rise of Hitler in Germany and was rooted in two beliefs: that Versailles had been unjust to the Germans, especially in its reparations clauses; and that France was pursuing a selfish and ultimately self-defeating policy of revenge and predominance which was inimical to the establishment of a genuine peace. Such a peace, they believed, could be brought about only through conciliation and cooperation. Thus, on the part of many Englishmen, appeasement involved an anti-French as well as a pro-German element.

When Hitler came to power in 1933, a discernible but weak reaction occurred against the pro-Germanism of more than a decade. The prevailing attitude was expressed by a Labour Party leader, who declared in the summer of 1933: "It serves us right! Had we revised Versailles and helped Germany out of her position of inequality and her economic difficulties in time, the Nazis would never have gained power." This guilt feeling persisted, though it was somewhat eroded as Hitler gradually revised Versailles by unilateral action, and was coupled with a strong pacifist movement along with a misunderstanding of Hitler and the nature of Nazism. Englishmen, even those who had read *Mein Kampf*, assumed that Hitler would become more moderate with the acquisition of political power and mass support, just as many a British radical had been sobered by the responsibilities of office. Moreover, in the ideological battles of the 'thirties Hitler's claim to be defending the West from Communism gained him a sympathetic audience, and not among conservatives alone. Labour Party leaders and liberals as well as conservatives fell under the spell of his propaganda, and eminent Englishmen who visited him became convinced that he was not only a bulwark against Bolshevism, but an essentially peace-loving man who had no other objective than that of unifying the Germans and making Germany a strong, vigorous nation capable of taking its rightful place among equals. Finally, since the unification of the Germans meant revision of frontiers (because Versailles had left many Germans outside the Reich's borders), the accepted Wilsonian principle of the right of self-determination worked in Hitler's favor. The appeasers, therefore, thought to bring about an era of peace and good will through economic cooperation, frontier revisions, and equality of status, all to be accomplished peaceably by the exercise of reasonableness and fair play.

Basically, the methods and objectives of the appeasers were laudatory and unexceptionable, given a world in which all nations subscribed to the same rules. But as Hitler and his contemporary Mussolini defied convention and adopted brusque, unilateral means of achieving equality of armament, expansion, and intervention in Austria and Spain, prominent men like Winston Churchill and Anthony Eden, and foreign office officials like Sir Robert Vansittart questioned the wisdom of appeasement. Increasingly and ever more vigorously they began to urge that since Britain was facing wilful aggressors rather than reasonable statesmen, the country must rearm and must build up an alliance, including Soviet Russia, in order to meet force with force. This challenge to the policy of appeasement began to grow perceptibly after Hitler's Rhineland coup of 1936, and rapidly gained strength after the *Anschluss* in March 1938. Nevertheless, Neville Chamberlain, who became Prime Minister in June 1937, and his closest advisers remained convinced that they could "do business" with Hitler and with Mussolini as well, and that they could achieve the genuinely peaceful world on which appeasers since the end of the First World War had set their hearts.

France, too, by 1936 was in the process of adopting an appeasement policy, but for reasons different from England's. Throughout the 1920's and up to the remilitarization of the Rhineland by Hitler in 1936, France had staunchly defended the provisions of the Versailles Treaty through her own strength and a coalition of powers who, like herself, would be endangered by a treaty revision— notably Belgium, Poland, and Czechoslovakia. France had been unable, however, to hold the line inflexibly and had agreed in 1932 to the virtual ending of reparations and to the principle of German arms equality. After that, the effects of the economic depression and of political scandals bringing governmental instability, popular unrest, and eventually the advent of Blum's Popular Front government in June 1936 weakened and divided France. In a last gesture of traditional diplomacy France had entered into an alliance with Soviet Russia in 1935 as an additional makeweight to the growing strength of Germany, but this move served only to exacerbate the growing division between Left and Right in France. "Better Hitler than Blum!" "Better Berlin than Moscow!" were slogans that revealed fertile soil for the seeds of Nazi propaganda.

The first French moves towards appeasement, however, had been directed towards Italy in connection with the Ethiopian adventure of 1935, and were motivated by the hope of keeping Mussolini in the anti-German camp. They failed when, despite the sanctions imposed by the League of Nations, Mussolini conquered Ethiopia and then, along with Hitler, intervened in the Spanish Civil War which broke out in 1936.

French internal weakness, such cracks in the former alliance structure as the coolness of Poland after its rapprochement with Germany in 1934, the Belgian declaration of neutrality in 1936, and a strong current of pacifism led successive French governments, beginning with Léon Blum's, into the path of German appeasement. This modification of the earlier French policy of resistance to revisionism enabled France and Great Britain to draw together in a renewed entente, this time with the latter in the lead. Together they maintained the policy of non-intervention in Spain; they sought to mollify Mussolini, and to bring about economic cooperation among the European nations in an effort to reduce the causes of irritation and aggression among the "have-nots." They both tended to discount the League of Nations after the Ethiopian failure, although the French, with their alliance system, even if moribund, placed greater emphasis upon the concept of collective security. While the German annexation of Austria in March 1938 led to a strengthening of Anglo-French ties, the virtual dependence of France on Great Britain meant that, short of a diplomatic revolution, they would both pursue much the same policy in the Czechoslovak crisis which ensued.

The background of that crisis lay in the conflict between the predominant Czechs and the Sudeten Germans who lived in the regions along the frontier. Undoubtedly this minority of about 3,200,000 had legitimate grievances, especially during the economic depression of the 1930's, even though legally they enjoyed the same political and cultural rights as other citizens of the Republic. Many Sudeten Germans, the so-called "Activists," worked with the government in order to achieve their objectives by political means. The efforts of the Czech government to reach agreement with the Sudeten Germans were begun seriously in 1936, but progress was slow. The rise of the Sudeten National Socialist Party seriously hampered discussions. Under the leadership of Konrad Henlein, who had been clandestinely in touch with Berlin since 1934, the Sudeten National Socialists were ever escalating their demands. Little by little Henlein emerged as a true Nazi whose demands meant, in effect, the right of self-determination and, in view of the characteristic abuse of Czechoslovakia in the Nazi press, ultimate union with the Reich. The agitation of the Henleinists rose to dangerous heights in the summer of 1938 when the relationship between Hitler and Henlein was revealed by their meetings and Hitler's vociferous public support of the Sudeten German cause.

The European nations had recognized the dangers in the situation from the time of the Austro-German *Anschluss* in March. Great Britain and France urged the Czechs to make a satisfactory settlement with the Sudetens, sending Lord Runciman in August to undertake mediation, but they found by September that the issue was not a domestic but an international one. At Nuremberg on September 12, Hitler demanded the right of self-determination for the Sudeten Germans, whom he represented as maltreated and persecuted by the Czechs, and declared that the Reich would support them in their efforts to obtain that right. There followed in quick succession the events that led to Munich: Berchtesgaden, the Anglo-French demand that Czechoslovakia give up the predominantly German areas, Godesberg, mobilizations, Hitler's announced determination to march into Czechoslovakia if Prague did not yield, and his agreement at the eleventh hour to a conference. At Munich Hitler obtained almost all that he had demanded; the agreement left Czechoslovakia a truncated and defenseless state.

In view of the "appeasement" of Hitler at Munich, the question is why, after almost five years of Hitler's broken promises, acts of defiance, and verbal threats, the British and French governments continued to attempt conciliation in the hope that they could still bring about peace in Europe and avoid the horrors of another war.

Three general answers may be identified: (1) The British and French governments blundered; (2) They deliberately planned or plotted the Munich settlement in order to turn Hitler eastward towards Soviet Russia; or (3) they had no other choice but to yield, of "tragic necessity," to Hitler's demands because they were too weak to risk war. These answers are not mutually exclusive and seldom does a student of the Munich crisis distinguish among them. An analysis of subsidiary questions reveals the overlapping of explanations.

Was Chamberlain, because of ignorance or egotism or stubbornness, led to the Munich Agreement by a failure to perceive that the assumptions of appeasement were no longer valid? Did he make a mistake, in other words, because he failed correctly to assess Hitler and his aims? Did Bonnet and Daladier blunder in their failure to make the most of their alliance with Russia? Did all three of them, led by anti-Communist sentiments or mistrust of the Soviets, blind themselves to the possibilities of creating a powerful coalition that would have stopped Hitler? If they had stood up to Hitler, would he have backed down? If a good case that he would have done so can be made from the evidence, then France and Britain clearly blundered.

Explanation of Munich as a plot or conspiracy assumes that the answer to the last two questions above is yes, and that with full knowledge of the situation and with a correct assessment of Hitler and his motives, Chamberlain, Bonnet, and Daladier deliberately gave him a free hand in Eastern Europe, beginning with the sacrifice of Czechoslovakia, in order to turn him against Soviet Russia and thus gain security for their own countries. The allegation of a conspiracy arose at the time of Munich and was elaborated by Communists and pro-Soviet interpreters when the publication of certain documents revealed the attitude of suspicion and mistrust of the U.S.S.R. held by the Western statesmen. The question immediately arises, however, whether men like Chamberlain and Daladier were capable of such Machiavellianism, and whether other interpretations are more consistent with what we know of their character and personality. Had even Bonnet, intriguer though he was alleged to be, deliberately plotted to turn Hitler eastward? In other words, did the refusal to accept Soviet proposals for collaboration and the exclusion of Russia from the Munich settlement prove that Britain and France were plotting against her? And if they had collaborated with Russia, would the Soviets have lived up to their promises? If so, then the Western statesmen blundered, but here is another "if" of history which cannot be verified because Soviet Russia was never put to the test.

Finally, the conclusion that Munich was a "tragic necessity" involves more factors than military weakness. Given the overwhelming desire of Frenchmen and Englishmen to avoid war, how could any responsible government, even if it wanted to do so, run the risk of conflict? Was not the will, even more than weapons, lacking for a confrontation with Nazi Germany? But, again, why were the people so lacking in comprehension of what was at stake? Was it because France and England lacked able and clear-sighted leadership, not just in 1938, but also in the years before the Munich crisis? Some writers—although they are not represented in the selections to follow, because of lack of space —have suggested that by 1938 the ruling classes of Britain and France were decadent and hence too weak to exert the necessary leadership. Whatever the answers to the why of Munich, the role of personalities, as well as the temper of the times and the military situation, must be taken into account.

Something of the character and personality of the British Prime Minister and of his critics shines through the British parliamentary speeches with which the selections on the contemporary conflict of views begin. Whatever

the divergence of outlook and attitude between the two sides, the earnestness and sincerity of Chamberlain and his opponents cannot be doubted. On the other hand, the debate in France turned to a far greater extent upon the veracity and the reliability of Georges Bonnet. Although he wrote his defense of French policy some seven years after Munich, his memoirs may properly be regarded as contemporary, for he based them upon his own documents and presented the views that we know from other sources he held in 1938. While all apologias like Bonnet's must be subjected to critical analysis, the testimony of such contemporaries as Pertinax and of another fellow countryman, Henri Noguères, later on, emphasize the necessity of scrutinizing Bonnet's explanation of Munich with more than usual care.

Coming to the historical studies of Munich, we find that, in the thirty years that have elapsed since then, published documents and memoirs have greatly widened and deepened our knowledge of both men and events. Furthermore, time has dampened the passions that Munich aroused and has thus enabled students, even those whose own memories go back to the crisis, to assess the evidence and to draw conclusions with greater wisdom and perspective. The same questions and issues that were debated at the time, however, continue to hold the center of interest.

The value of perspective emerges from the study of appeasement by Martin Gilbert, for he finds that while elements underlying the older appeasement remained, that of the Munich Agreement was new and was motivated mainly by fear rather than by confidence and hope. The other selections in Part II deal with one or more of the three general answers to "Why Munich" that have been suggested above, but sometimes more implicitly than explicitly. Inevitably Chamberlain occupies a central position. He is praised by Iain Macleod, his policy is explained by D. C. Watt as partly the result of Dominion attitudes, and he is implicitly criticized by J. W. Wheeler-Bennett, who also includes the French statesmen in his characterization of the leading actors in the drama of Munich. A lengthier treatment of the French is offered by Henri Noguères, who returns essentially to the position of Pertinax and condemns Bonnet and his colleagues for errors of omission and commission which almost add up to betrayal and treachery. On the other hand, Arnold Toynbee's interpretation of Chamberlain and his relations with Hitler and France offers a more kindly but nonetheless critical view, based upon assumptions that differ from those of either Noguères or Andrew Rothstein. Toynbee fails to find any conspiracy, whereas Rothstein flatly accuses both Britain and France of it. Keith Eubank, taking still another viewpoint, supports the contemporary plea of "tragic necessity," adding the dimension of willpower omitted by such apologists as Bonnet. Finally, William L. Shirer's study of the German plot to overthrow Hitler, which was seized upon by Munich critics as additional proof that Britain and France had badly blundered, suggests that the probability of its implementation was not great, but concludes that Munich was not a necessity even though Hitler was not bluffing.

In conclusion, Eubank's summary of the "myth" of Munich helps both to dispel the misconceptions about diplomacy which it has engendered and also to raise the question of what good it does to probe into such historical events as the Munich crisis. If history is what people believe to be true, as may well be argued, then the "Munich" of our current vocabulary represents the truth for all practical purposes. On the other hand, we are still living in a world of both bloody and ideological conflicts, and although the exact duplicate of the Czechoslovak crisis and the events leading to the Munich Agreement will never recur, still there are problems sufficiently similar so that assessing the factors which explain Munich may help to enlighten us in solving similar crises.

Finally, perhaps Munich reveals the nemesis of previous policy rather than merely the blunders or necessities of 1938. Munich may be well worth studying in order to show the need for clear vision and the importance of long-term planning of national policy upon the bases of critical and ever-revised analyses of conditions and peoples. Although hindsight is admittedly much clearer than foresight, nevertheless there is no hope for peaceful international relations unless men seek to avoid the pitfalls of ignorance and opinionated judgment that surrounded Munich.

CHRONOLOGY OF THE MUNICH CRISIS—1938

FEBRUARY 20 In a public speech, Hitler promised protection to German minorities outside the Reich.

MARCH 13 Union of Austria with Germany was proclaimed.
14 Germany assured Prague of its desire to improve German-Czech relations. France and Russia declared that they would honor their treaty obligations to aid Czechoslovakia, if attacked.
17 Litvinov, the Soviet foreign minister, proposed concerted action among the powers to stop further aggression.
24 Prime Minister Chamberlain, in the House of Commons, rejected Litvinov's proposal, avoided any forthright commitments, but did assert that if war broke out Great Britain might become involved.

APRIL 24 Konrad Henlein, leader of the Sudeten National Socialist Party, stated his eight-point program at Karlsbad, demanding among other things full equality of status for Germans, full autonomy for German areas, and freedom for the Germans to adhere to "the ideology of Germans." A few days later he visited London and Berlin; upon his return disorders began to break out in German areas.
29 The French and British premiers and foreign ministers, meeting in London, agreed to use their influence to bring about a peaceful solution of the Sudeten German question; on May 7 the two governments advised the Prague government to make greater concessions than those that Premier Hodža had proposed.

MAY 20–21 The "May crisis." Rumors of German troop concentrations led the Prague government to mobilize 400,000 men. France and Britain took a strong stand, and Germany denied any troop movements directed against Czechoslovakia.
28 Hitler secretly ordered the preparation of plans for action against Czechoslovakia by October 2, the strengthening of fortifications on the French border, and a large increase in the air force.

JUNE–JULY Negotiations took place between the Sudeten leaders and the Czechoslovak government, which published a draft nationality statute, July 26, that fell short of Henlein's Karlsbad demands.

AUGUST 3 Lord Runciman arrived in Prague to undertake mediation.

SEPTEMBER 1 Henlein submitted to Hitler a compromise proposal for cantonal self-determination, worked out by Runciman, but Hitler flatly rejected the plan.
6 The Czechoslovak government issued its "Fourth Plan," providing that all nationalities share proportionately in state offices, enterprises, and other organizations. The Sudeten leaders broke off negotiations (Sept. 7) because of disorders at Moravská Ostrava, and thereafter extremists resorted increasingly to violence.
12 At Nuremberg Hitler demanded that the Sudeten Germans be given the right of self-determination, thus heightening the sense of crisis.
13 Czechoslovakia proclaimed martial law in the districts affected by Nazi-inspired violence.
15 The Hitler-Chamberlain meeting at Berchtesgaden. Hitler declared that the Sudeten Germans must "return" to the Reich and that he would help them even at the risk of war.

16   Runciman returned to London and recommended, among other points, that frontier districts where the Germans were in a majority should be given the right of self-determination.

18–19   Daladier and Bonnet in London agreed with the British ministers to urge Czechoslovakia to accede to Hitler's terms, offering an international guarantee of the truncated state.

20   The Czechoslovak government proposed arbitration on the basis of the Locarno Treaty of 1925, but France and Britain flatly rejected this offer as inadequate.

21   Prague yielded under French and British pressure; the cabinet resigned the next day and General Jan Sirový formed a new government, which ordered full mobilization on the 23rd.

22–24   Chamberlain-Hitler meetings at Godesberg. Hitler insisted upon the German occupation of districts to be ceded to the Reich by October 1; Czech military withdrawal without destroying or removing "military, commercial, or traffic establishments"; and other demands not mentioned at Berchtesgaden, which "shocked" Chamberlain, who obtained a memorandum of Hitler's terms.

24   France ordered partial mobilization.

25   Czechoslovakia rejected the Godesberg memorandum.

25–26   The French and British ministers conferred in London. The French insisted they would honor their treaty obligations and the British promised to lend support if France became engaged in hostilities with Germany.

26   Chamberlain sent Sir Horace Wilson to Hitler, urging a conference. Hitler rejected the plea and told the Italian ambassador that he would march at 2 P.M. on the 28th; at the Sports Palace in the evening Hitler declared that his Godesberg demands represented a minimum.

27   Wilson again met Hitler and warned that if war came, Britain would support France. The news of the British promise was published, but the communiqué from London was dubbed "unofficial" by Bonnet. Hitler's decision to march by 2 P.M. the next day, if Prague did not yield, was also published. Chamberlain's speech in the evening still held out hope of negotiations. Roosevelt urged a peaceful settlement. Britain ordered mobilization of the fleet.

28   In response to representations by the British, French, and Italian ambassadors, Hitler agreed to a four-power conference at Munich on the following day.

29   The Munich conference reached agreement at 1 A.M. on the 30th, providing that: Czechoslovakia should cede to Germany Sudeten German territory, evacuating it between October 1 and 10 "without any existing installations having been destroyed"; and Germany would begin occupation of the predominantly German territory on October 1. An international commission would lay down the details of evacuation, would determine the territories in which a plebiscite was to be held, and would make the final determination of frontiers.

30   Chamberlain and Hitler signed a declaration "that the question of Anglo-German relations is of the first importance for the two countries and for Europe . . . and we are determined to continue our efforts to remove possible sources of difference and thus to contribute to assure the peace of Europe."

CONFLICT OF OPINION

What is the alternative to this bleak and barren policy of the inevitability of war? In my view it is that we should seek by all means in our power to avoid war, by analyzing possible causes, by trying to remove them, by discussion in a spirit of collaboration and good will.

——NEVILLE CHAMBERLAIN

Between submission and immediate war there was this third alternative [a combination of powers including Russia], which gave a hope not only of peace but of justice. It is quite true that such a policy in order to succeed demanded that Britain should declare straight out and a long time beforehand that she would, with others, join to defend Czechoslovakia against an unprovoked aggression. His Majesty's Government refused to give that guarantee when it would have saved the situation," . . .

——WINSTON CHURCHILL

Thus, on the eve of the Munich meeting the French government did not at all envisage a precarious entente with Germany, made with Czechoslovakia as scapegoat. It hoped for a general accord established among *all* the countries of our continent, which would save Europe from ruin and chaos, fatal consequences of a new war.

——GEORGES BONNET

[Bonnet] exercised all his ingenuity to destroy our alliances, the only brake we could apply to Hitler's progress. . . . He turned the Munich Conference into a boundless diplomatic disaster.

——PERTINAX

This was the gravamen of the contemporary charge against Chamberlain's appeasement; not that conciliation was wrong, or that Treaty revision was wrong, as general guidelines for a liberal and Christian policy, but that such a base was unrealistic when applied to Nazi Germany in 1938.

——MARTIN GILBERT

Either there had to be concessions or else we had to go to war. But how *could* we go to war, when we ourselves were unready, when the French were blowing hot and cold, when the Russians could not be relied upon, and when the Dominions—South Africa, Australia and Canada—were divided?

——IAIN MACLEOD

Hitler's blindness to the truth about Chamberlain remained as dense down to 15 March 1939 as Chamberlain's blindness to the truth about Hitler remained down to the 18th of the same month. . . .

——ARNOLD J. TOYNBEE

Was the Franco-British surrender at Munich necessary? Was Adolf Hitler not bluffing? The answer, paradoxically, to both questions, we now know, is No.

——WILLIAM L. SHIRER

There was an ever-increasing disparity between their [Daladier's and Bonnet's] words and their deeds, for while they spoke of the obligations that France had undertaken they never stopped acting in such a manner that they would not have to fulfill them.

——HENRI NOGUÈRES

The British and French Governments acted as they did in 1938 because they hoped, by handing over Czechoslovakia to Hitler, to keep the door open for him to commit further aggression in the east of Europe, preferably against the U.S.S.R.

——ANDREW ROTHSTEIN

The non-appeasers offer a glib, facile explanation for the Munich Agreement because they cannot see the entire story in all of its tragedy. . . . It was a story of free men who were unprepared to wage war against the tyrant! This was the truth of the Munich Agreement.

——KEITH EUBANK

I. CONTEMPORARY CONFLICTS OF OPINION

THE BRITISH PARLIAMENTARY DEBATE

The Czechoslovak crisis and the Munich settlement raised a storm of controversy within the Western nations. Nowhere was the government's policy more hotly debated than in Great Britain where the House of Commons became a forum for the discussion of the pros and cons of the Agreement. While the tradition of parliamentary courtesy tended to obscure the passions beneath the arguments, it permitted a clear confrontation over the issues. It should be noted, however, that no one deplored the peaceful outcome of the crisis or argued that Britain should have gone to war. The excerpts below are taken from the record of the three-day debate and represent the views of such proponents of the government as Chamberlain and Sir Samuel Hoare, and such critics as Duff Cooper, Clement Attlee, and Winston Churchill.

DUFF COOPER, HOUSE OF COMMONS,
OCTOBER 3, 1938.

THE debate in the British House of Commons on the Munich agreement was opened on October 3, 1938, by Duff Cooper who had resigned his post as First Lord of the Admiralty. After explaining how painful it was for him to resign in protest over the Munich policy, he continued:]

I have always been a student of foreign politics. I have served 10 years in the Foreign Office, and I have studied the history of this and of other countries, and I have always believed that one of the most important principles in foreign policy and the conduct of foreign policy should be to make your policy plain to other countries, to let them know where you stand and what in certain circumstances you are prepared to do. . . .

I believe that the great defect in our foreign policy during recent months and recent weeks has been that we have failed to do so. During the last four weeks we have been drifting, day by day, nearer into war with Germany, and we have never said, until the last moment, and

then in most uncertain terms, that we were prepared to fight. We knew that information to the opposite effect was being poured into the ears of the head of the German State. He had been assured, reassured, and fortified in the opinion that in no case would Great Britain fight. . . .

I had urged . . . after the rape of Austria, that Great Britain should make a firm declaration of what her foreign policy was, and then and later I was met with this, that the people of this country are not prepared to fight for Czechoslovakia. . . .

I besought my colleagues not to see this problem always in terms of Czechoslovakia, not to review it always from the difficult strategic position of that small country, but rather to say to themselves, "A moment may come when, owing to the invasion of Czechoslovakia, a European war will begin, and when that moment comes we must take part in that war, we cannot keep out of it, and there is no doubt upon which side we shall fight. Let the world know that and it will give those who are prepared to disturb the peace reason to hold their

From *Parliamentary Debates*, 5th series, vol. 339 (1938), cols 30, 31–34, 39, 40, 47–52, 54, 56–58, 62–63, 150–154, 162, 360–369, 373, 548–553.

hand." It is perfectly true that after the assault on Austria the Prime Minister made a speech in this House—an excellent speech with every word of which I was in complete agreement—and what he said then was repeated and supported by the Chancellor of the Exchequer at Lanark. It was, however, a guarded statement. It was a statement to the effect that if there were such a war it would be unwise for anybody to count upon the possibility of our staying out.

That is not the language which the dictators understand. Together with new methods and a new morality they have introduced also a new vocabulary into Europe. They have discarded the old diplomatic methods of correspondence. . . . I had hoped that it might be possible to make a statement to Herr Hitler before he made his speech at Nuremberg. On all sides we were being urged to do so by people in this country, by Members in this House, by Leaders of the Opposition, by the Press, by the heads of foreign States, even by Germans who were supporters of the regime and did not wish to see it plunged into a war which might destroy it. But we were always told that on no account must we irritate Herr Hitler; it was particularly dangerous to irritate him before he made a public speech, because if he were so irritated he might say some terrible things from which afterwards there would be no retreat. It seems to me that Herr Hitler never makes a speech save under the influence of considerable irritation, and the addition of one more irritant would not, I should have thought, have made a great difference, whereas the communication of a solemn fact would have produced a sobering effect.

After the chance of Nuremberg was missed I had hoped that the Prime Minister at his first interview with Herr Hitler at Berchtesgaden would make the position plain, but he did not do so. Again, at Godesberg I had hoped that that statement would be made in unequivocal language. Again I was disappointed. Hitler had another speech to make in Berlin. Again an opportunity occurred of telling him exactly where we

stood before he made that speech, but again the opportunity was missed, and it was only after the speech that he was informed. . . .

Then came the last appeal from the Prime Minister on Wednesday morning. For the first time from the beginning to the end of the four weeks of negotiations Herr Hitler was prepared to yield an inch, an ell perhaps, but to yield some measure to the representations of Great Britain. But I would remind the House that the message from the Prime Minister was not the first news that he had received that morning. At dawn he had learned of the mobilisation of the British Fleet. It is impossible to know what are the motives of man and we shall probably never be satisfied as to which of these two sources of inspiration moved him most when he agreed to go to Munich, but we do know that never before had he given in and that then he did. I had been urging the mobilisation of the Fleet for many days. I had thought that this was the kind of language which would be easier for Herr Hitler to understand than the guarded language of diplomacy or the conditional clauses of the Civil Service. I had urged that something in that direction might be done at the end of August and before the Prime Minister went to Berchtesgaden. I had suggested that it should accompany the mission of Sir Horace Wilson. I remember the Prime Minister stating it was the one thing that would ruin that mission, and I said it was the one thing that would lead it to success.

That is the deep difference between the Prime Minister and myself throughout these days. The Prime Minister has believed in addressing Herr Hitler through the language of sweet reasonableness. I have believed that he was more open to the language of the mailed fist. . . .

The Prime Minister has confidence in the good will and in the word of Herr Hitler, although when Herr Hitler broke the Treaty of Versailles he undertook to keep the Treaty of Locarno, and when· he broke the Treaty of Locarno he undertook not to interfere further, or to have further territorial aims, in Europe. When he entered Austria by force he authorised his henchmen to give an authoritative assurance that he would not interfere with Czechoslovakia. That was less than six months ago. Still, the Prime Minister believes that he can rely upon the good faith of Hitler; he believes that Hitler is interested only in Germany, as the Prime Minister was assured. . . .

The Prime Minister may be right. I can assure you, Mr. Speaker, with the deepest sincerity, that I hope and pray that he is right, but I cannot believe what he believes. I wish I could. . . . I remember when we were discussing the Godesberg ultimatum that I said that if I were a party to persuading, or even to suggesting to, the Czechoslovak Government that they should accept that ultimatum, I should never be able to hold up my head again. . . . I have ruined, perhaps, my political career. But that is a little matter; I have retained something which is to me of great value—I can still walk about the world with my head erect.

PRIME MINISTER NEVILLE CHAMBER-
LAIN, HOUSE OF COMMONS,
OCTOBER 3, 1938.

[After making some remarks on the other participants at the Munich Conference, and attributing a "constantly increasing influence" to the United States, he continued:]

In my view the strongest force of all, one which grew and took fresh shapes and forms every day was the force not of any one individual, but was that unmistakable sense of unanimity among the peoples of the world that war somehow must be averted. The peoples of the British Empire were at one with those of Germany, of France and of Italy, and their anxiety, their intense desire for peace, pervaded the whole atmosphere of the conference, and I believe that that, and not threats, made possible the concessions that were made. . . .

Ever since I assumed my present office my main purpose has been to work for the pacification of Europe, for the removal of those suspicions and those animosities which have so long poisoned the air. The path which leads to appeasement is long and bristles with obstacles. The question of Czechoslovakia is the latest and perhaps the most dangerous. Now that we have got past it, I feel that it may be possible to make further progress along the road to sanity.

My right hon. Friend [Duff Cooper] has alluded in somewhat bitter terms to my conversation last Friday morning with Herr Hitler. I do not know why that conversation should give rise to suspicion, still less to criticism. I entered into no pact. I made no new commitments. There is no secret understanding. Our conversation was hostile to no other nation. The objects of that conversation, for which I asked, was to try to extend a little further the personal contact which I had established with Herr Hitler and which I believe to be essential in modern diplomacy. We had a friendly and entirely non-committal conversation, carried on, on my part, largely with a view to seeing whether there could be points in common between the head of a democratic Government and the ruler of a totalitarian State. We see the result in the declaration which has been published, in which my right hon. Friend finds so much ground for suspicion. . . .

[After quoting the declaration which he had signed with Hitler, and briefly commenting upon the text, Chamberlain continued:]

I believe there are many who will feel with me that such a declaration, signed by the German Chancellor and myself, is something more than a pious expression of opinion. In our relations with other countries everything depends upon there being sincerity and good will on both sides. I believe that there is sincerity and good will on both sides in this declaration. That is why to me its significance goes far beyond its actual words. If there is one lesson which we should learn from the events of these last weeks it is this, that lasting peace is not to be obtained by sitting still and waiting for it to come. It requires active, positive efforts to achieve it. No doubt I shall have plenty of critics who will say that I am guilty of facile optimism, and that

I should disbelieve every word that is uttered by rulers of other great States in Europe. I am too much of a realist to believe that we are going to achieve our paradise in a day. We have only laid the foundations of peace. The superstructure is not even begun. . . .

While we must renew our determination to fill up the deficiencies that yet remain in our armaments and in our defensive precautions, so that we may be ready to defend ourselves and make our diplomacy effective—[*Interruption*] —yes I am a realist—nevertheless I say with an equal sense of reality that I do see fresh opportunities of approaching this subject of disarmament opening up before us, and I believe that they are at least as hopeful to-day as they have been at any previous time. It is to such tasks— the winning back of confidence, the gradual removal of hostility between nations until they feel that they can safely discard their weapons, one by one, that I would wish to devote what energy and time may be left to me before I hand over my office to younger men.

CLEMENT ATTLEE, HOUSE OF COMMONS,
OCTOBER 3, 1938.

[Mr. Clement Attlee, head of the Labour Party and leader of the opposition in the House of Commons, followed the Prime Minister in the debate of October 3, 1938:]

We all feel relief that war has not come this time. Every one of us has been passing through days of anxiety; we cannot, however, feel that peace has been established, but that we have nothing but an armistice in a state of war. We have been unable to go in for care-free rejoicing. We have felt that we are in the midst of a tragedy. We have felt humiliation. This has not been a victory for reason and humanity. It has been a victory for brute force. At every stage of the proceedings there have been time limits laid down by the owner and ruler of armed force. The terms have not been terms negotiated; they have been terms laid down as ultimata. We have seen to-day a gallant, civilised and democratic people betrayed and handed over to a ruthless despotism. We have seen something more. We have seen the cause of democracy, which is, in our view, the cause of civilisation and humanity, receive a terrible defeat.

I think that in the mind of every thoughtful person in this country when he heard that this settlement had been arrived at at Munich, there was a conflict. On the one hand there was enormous relief that war had been averted, at all events for the time being; on the other, there was a sense of humiliation and foreboding for the future. . . .

The events of these last few days constitute one of the greatest diplomatic defeats that this country and France have ever sustained. There can be no doubt that it is a tremendous victory for Herr Hitler. Without firing a shot, by the mere display of military force, he has achieved a dominating position in Europe which Germany failed to win after four years of war. He has overturned the balance of power in Europe. He has destroyed the last fortress of democracy in Eastern Europe which stood in the way of his ambition. He has opened his way to the food, the oil and the resources which he requires in order to consolidate his military power, and he has successfully defeated and reduced to impotence the forces that might have stood against the rule of violence.

The Prime Minister has given us an account of his actions. Everybody recognises the great exertions he has made in the cause of peace. When the captain of a ship by disregarding all rules of navigation has gone right off his course and run the ship into great danger, watchers from the shore, naturally impressed with the captain's frantic efforts to try to save something from the shipwreck, cheer him when he comes ashore and even want to give him a testimonial, but there follows an inquiry, an inquest, on the victims, and the question will be asked how the vessel got so far off its course, how and why it was so hazarded? All the faults of seamanship and errors of judgment must be brought to light, and no amount of devotion at the eleventh hour will save that captain from the verdict that he has hazarded his ship through bad seamanship. Parliament is the grand inquest of the British nation, and it is our duty to inquire not alone into the actions of the Prime Minister during the last few days or the last few weeks, but into the whole course of policy which has brought this country into such great danger and such great anxiety....

I want to turn now to the cause of the crisis which we have undergone. The cause was not the existence of minorities in Czechoslovakia; it was not that the position of the Sudeten Germans had become intolerable. It was not the wonderful principle of self-determination. It was because Herr Hitler had decided that the time was ripe for another step forward in his design to dominate Europe. I think it is necessary to be clear on this, because the Prime Minister seems to me to be laying a great deal too much stress on the anxiety of Herr Hitler for his fellow-Germans in Czechoslovakia. I have no doubt that has been so, but it did not become intense until about two years ago. It was quite a minor matter, and I fear that the Prime Minister is deceived if he thinks that the cause of this trouble has been the woes of the Sudeten Germans. I say that the question of the Sudeten Germans has been used as a counter in the game of politics, and in other conditions Herr Hitler might just as well have used the people of Memel, the people of South Denmark, the people in the Trentino or the Germans in South Tyrol....

The history of the last seven years is the background of this crisis, and the first point I must make to the Government is this. This crisis did not come unexpectedly. It was obvious to any intelligent student of foreign affairs that this attack would come. The immediate signal was given by the Prime Minister himself on 7th March of this year when he said: "What country in Europe today if threatened by a larger Power can rely upon the League for protection? None." It was at once an invitation to Herr Hitler and a confession of the failure of the Government. The invitation was accepted a few days later by the An-

schluss in Austria. Then our Government and the French Government could have faced the consequences. They could have told Czechoslovakia "We cannot any longer defend you. You had better now make the best terms you can with Germany, enter her political orbit and give her anything to escape before the wrath comes upon you." But they did nothing of the sort. Czechoslovakia continued under the supposed shelter of these treaties. True, it was urged that something should be done for the Sudeten Germans but there was no attempt made to take early steps to prevent this aggression....

I heard a suggestion from the benches opposite. "What about the U.S.S.R.?" Throughout the whole of these proceedings the U.S.S.R. has stood by its pledges and its declarations and there has been some pretty hard lying about it, too. There have been lies told, and people knew they were lies, about alleged conversations between M. Litvinoff and the French Foreign Minister. At no time has there been any difficulty in knowing where the U.S.S.R. stood. At no time has there been any consultation. I am aware that the Prime Minister may say that we were not the prime factor in this problem and that we were only concerned after France had been brought into it. But we have had very close collaboration with France, and in the order of commitment the U.S.S.R. comes before this country, and it has been a very great weakness that throughout there has been this cold-shouldering of the U.S.S.R....

When the National Government overthrew the whole policy of collective security and abandoned it and the League, we told this House over and over again that we were entering on a very dangerous course. We realised that we were back in 1914 with all its dangers, and we knew that sooner or later a challenge would come to this country; and that is what has happened. The real pith of it is that, having decided to leave the League system which we practised and in which we believed, and to embark on a policy of alliances and power politics, instead of strengthening the people whose natural interests were with ours, we have had nothing but constant flirtations with this and that dictator. The Prime Minister has been the dupe of the dictators, and I say that to-day we are in a dangerous position.

SIR SAMUEL HOARE, SECRETARY OF STATE FOR THE HOME DEPARTMENT, HOUSE OF COMMONS, OCTOBER 3, 1938.
... A week ago we were on the verge of a terrible abyss. The Hon. Member for Bishop Auckland (Mr. Dalton), who has just sat down, seemed to have forgotten the position in which we were then placed. The speech that he has just made seemed to take little account of the fact that a few days ago we were within a hair's breadth of the greatest catastrophe that the world has ever seen. Did we shrink from it in fear, or did we feel that there was some hope still of finding a path round it to more solid ground? I am fully aware that there are some hon. Members, and some people in the country, who believe that no peace is possible in Europe as long as the dictatorships exist, who hold, quite sincerely, the view—I think the hon. Gentleman who has just sat down does—that as long as the dictatorships exist, war is inevitable, and that it may be better to have war now, when we have an issue that may be supposed to appeal to the whole world, rather than to put it off to some future date when our position may be more difficult and dangerous. ...

The conclusion of such a view is to me so appalling that I could not accept it if I thought there was still some glimmer of hope that the catastrophe might yet be averted. What is more important, the Prime Minister had that settled conviction. It was on that account that he made his superhuman efforts at great risk to himself, at great risk to the Government of which he is a member—but these things do not count in moments of this gravity—to take upon himself the responsibility of trying at the last moment to prevent this catastrophe coming upon us.

The Prime Minister acted not alone as the head of the Government of which I am a member. He acted rather as the spokesman of the millions of men and women from one end of the world to the other who were determined that we should still try to keep a controlling hand upon the course of events and avoid an appalling calamity that would undoubtedly have ended in the extinction of civilisation as we have known it. ... I claim that, having undertaken the responsibility of mediation, it would have been courting certain failure if at one and the same time when he was attempting to mediate he engaged himself upon a policy of threats and ultimatums.

That is the answer to the main charge of my right Hon. Friend the Member for St. George's, Westminster (Mr. Cooper) I claim that it would have met certain failure if at the very time when we were attempting to mediate and to obtain a peaceful settlement, we had accepted the advice of those who said you must face Herr Hitler with a public ultimatum. I go further, and I say that if we had made an ultimatum in the days immediately before the Nuremberg speech Europe would to-day have been plunged into a world war. ...

The hon. Gentleman opposite asked me specifically about Russia. He asked me why there was not closer consultation in these critical weeks with the Government of the Soviet Republic. That Government was under a Treaty obligation similar to that of France, and dependent upon it, to go to the assistance of Czechoslovakia in certain circumstances. The Russian guarantee was only to come into operation when the French guarantee was already operating. M. Litvinoff indicated, indeed he made a public declaration at Geneva on 21st September, that the Soviet Government was ready to give all possible help if France came to the assistance of Czechoslovakia. As I have explained, that is all that Russia was under Treaty bound to do. Her action would have been consequent upon that of France, and it was therefore natural that there should have been consultation, as in fact there was, between France and the Soviet Republic, and His Majesty's Government, in view of their different positions. We were content to let the French Government take the lead in consulting with the

Russian Government, whose position was analogous to theirs. To say, as the hon. Gentleman said, that the Soviet Republic was cold-shouldered is a complete exaggeration of the position. The Foreign Secretary had an exchange of views with the Soviet Ambassador before the latter left, and at Geneva the British delegates maintained the contact. The Soviet Ambassador was received again, quite recently, at the Foreign Office, after his return to London. So much for the hon. Member's question about our attitude towards the Soviet Republic.

War has been averted; has the price paid been too high? I frankly admit that Czechoslovakia has received a staggering blow. . . .

I say with all deliberation that, when once Germany rearmed and became powerful, and when once the Anschluss took place, the strategic frontier of the republic was turned. The Sudeten Germans looked to reunion with the Reich. [HON. MEMBERS: "Reunion?"] To union with the Reich. It was reunion with a German State. Union with the Reich was the ideal that they were determined to achieve. Further than that, we faced the fact that owing to the geographical position of Czechoslovakia it mattered not who might win or lose the war, Czechoslovakia would almost inevitably be destroyed. Some said it would be a matter of days and others said a matter of weeks, but all were agreed who had studied the strategic position that it could not be a matter of more than a month or two. In the meanwhile, the republic would have been destroyed; immense slaughter would have taken place within its boundaries; devastation would have run riot. Supposing that at the end of the war we emerged the victors—and I have always believed, as every Member in this House believes, that in the final result we should emerge the victors—then we should be confronted with a position in which Czechoslovakia as we know it to-day would have been destroyed, and I do not believe that the negotiators of the peace treaty in any conditions would ever recreate its old frontiers. . . .

The right hon. Gentleman the Leader of the Opposition, in a picturesque passage, spoke of the Prime Minister as the captain who had saved the ship which his bad seamanship had driven almost on to the rocks. When the time comes for the verdict to be given upon the Prime Minister's conduct, let me tell the right hon. Gentleman that none of us here fears that verdict. I believe that the criticisms to which we have listened in the House to-day very little represent the great body of feeling. I believe the great body of our fellow-citizens not only in this country but in the Dominions and in the whole Empire, are grateful to the Prime Minister for the efforts that he has made. They are grateful to the Prime Minister for having persistently sustained the policy of peace and mediation. They do not take the view that war is inevitable. They believe that under his wise guidance we may succeed in creating a new Europe in which men and women can go about their business in peace and security.

WINSTON CHURCHILL, HOUSE OF
COMMONS, OCTOBER 5, 1938.

[After refusing to pay tribute to the Prime Minister, but complimenting Duff Cooper and another speaker, Churchill launched into a vigorous criticism of Munich:]

Having thus fortified myself by the example of others, I will proceed to emulate them. I will, therefore, begin by saying the most unpopular and most unwelcome thing. I will begin by saying what everybody would like to ignore or forget but which must nevertheless be stated, namely, that we have sustained a total and unmitigated defeat, and that France has suffered even more than we have.

VISCOUNTESS ASTOR: Nonsense.

MR. CHURCHILL: When the Noble Lady cries "Nonsense," she could not have heard the Chancellor of the Exchequer [Sir John Simon] admit in his illuminating and comprehensive speech just now that Herr Hitler had gained in this particular leap forward in substance all he set out to gain. The utmost my right hon. Friend the Prime Minister has been able to secure by all his immense exertions, by all the great efforts and mobilisation which took place in this country, and by all the anguish and strain through which we have passed in this country, the utmost he has been able to gain—[HON. MEMBERS: "Is peace."] I thought I might be allowed to make that point in its due place, and I propose to deal with it. The utmost he has been able to gain for Czechoslovakia and in the matters which were in dispute has been that the German dictator, instead of snatching his victuals from the table, has been content to have them served to him course by course.

The Chancellor of the Exchequer said it was the first time Herr Hitler had been made to retract—I think that was the word—in any degree. We really must not waste time, after all this long Debate, upon the difference between the positions reached at Berchtesgaden, at Godesberg and at Munich. They can be very simply epitomised, if the House will permit me to vary the metaphor. £1 was demanded at the pistol's point. When it was given, £2 were demanded at the pistol's point. Finally, the dictator consented to take £1 17s. 6d. and the rest in promises of good will for the future.

Now I come to the point, which was mentioned to me just now from some quarters of the House, about the saving of peace. No one has been a more resolute and uncompromising struggler for peace than the Prime Minister. Everyone knows that. Never has there been such intense and undaunted determination to maintain and to secure peace. That is quite true. Nevertheless, I am not quite clear why there was so much danger of Great Britain or France being involved in a war with Germany at this juncture if, in fact, they were ready all along to sacrifice Czechoslovakia. The terms which the Prime Minister brought back with him—I quite agree at the last moment; everything had got off the rails and nothing but his intervention could have saved the peace, but I am talking of the events of the summer—could easily have been agreed, I believe,

through the ordinary diplomatic channels at any time during the summer. And I will say this, that I believe the Czechs, left to themselves and told they were going to get no help from the Western Powers, would have been able to make better terms than they have got—they could hardly have worse—after all this tremendous perturbation.

There never can be any absolute certainty that there will be a fight if one side is determined that it will give way completely. When one reads the Munich terms, when one sees what is happening in Czechoslovakia from hour to hour, when one is sure, I will not say of Parliamentary approval but of Parliamentary acquiescence, when the Chancellor of the Exchequer makes a speech which at any rate tries to put in a very powerful and persuasive manner the fact that, after all, it was inevitable and indeed righteous—right—when we saw all this, and everyone on this side of the House, including many Members of the Conservative Party who are supposed to be vigilant and careful guardians of the national interest, it is quite clear that nothing vitally affecting us was at stake, it seems to me that one must ask, What was all the trouble and fuss about? . . .

We are asked to vote for this Motion which has been put upon the Paper, and it is certainly a Motion couched in very uncontroversial terms, as, indeed, is the Amendment moved from the Opposition side. I cannot myself express my agreement with the steps which have been taken, and as the Chancellor of the Exchequer has put his side of the case with so much ability I will attempt, if I may be permitted, to put the case from a different angle. I have always held the view that the maintenance of peace depends upon the accumulation of deterrents against the aggressor, coupled with a sincere effort to redress grievances. Herr Hitler's victory, like so many of the famous struggles that have governed the fate of the world, was won upon the narrowest of margins. After the seizure of Austria in March we faced this problem in our Debates. I ventured to appeal to the Government to go a little further than the Prime Minister went, and to give a pledge that in conjunction with France and other Powers they would guarantee the security of Czechoslovakia while the Sudeten-Deutsch question was being examined either by a League of Nations Commission or some other impartial body, and I still believe that if that course had been followed events would not have fallen into this disastrous state. I agree very much with my right hon. Friend the Member for Sparkbrook (Mr. Amery) when he said on that occasion—I cannot remember his actual words—"Do one thing or the other; either say you will disinterest yourself in the matter altogether or take the step of giving a guarantee which will have the greatest chance of securing protection for that country."

France and Great Britain together, especially if they had maintained a close contact with Russia, which certainly was not done, would have been able in those days in the summer, when they had the prestige, to influence many of the smaller States of Europe, and I believe they could have determined the attitude of Poland. Such a combination, prepared at a time when the German dictator was not deeply and irrevocably committed to his new adventure, would, I believe, have given strength to all those forces in Germany which resisted this departure, this new design. They were varying forces, those of a military character which declared that Germany was not ready to undertake a world war, and all that mass of moderate opinion and popular opinion which dreaded war, and some elements of which still have some influence upon the German Government. Such action would have given strength to all that intense desire for peace which the helpless German masses share with their British and French fellow men, and which, as we have been reminded, found a passionate and rarely permitted vent in the joyous manifestations with which the Prime Minister was acclaimed in Munich.

All these forces, added to the other deterrents which combinations of Powers, great and small, ready to stand firm upon the front of law and for the ordered remedy of grievances, would have formed, might well have been effective. Of course you cannot say for certain that they would. [*Interruption.*] I try to argue fairly with the House. At the same time I do not think it is fair to charge those who wished to see this course followed, and followed consistently and resolutely, with having wished for an immediate war. Between submission and immediate war there was this third alternative, which gave a hope not only of peace but of justice. It is quite true that such a policy in order to succeed demanded that Britain should declare straight out and a long time beforehand that she would, with others, join to defend Czechoslovakia against an unprovoked aggression. His Majesty's Government refused to give that guarantee when it would have saved the situation, yet in the end they gave it when it was too late, and now, for the future, they renew it when they have not the slightest power to make it good.

All is over. Silent, mournful, abandoned, broken, Czechoslovakia recedes into the darkness. . . . No one has a right to say that the plebiscite which is to be taken in areas under Saar conditions, and the clean-cut of the 50 per cent. areas—that those two operations together amount in the slightest degree to a verdict of self-determination. It is a fraud and a farce to invoke that name.

We in this country, as in other Liberal and democratic countries, have a perfect right to exalt the principle of self-determination, but it comes ill out of the mouths of those in totalitarian States who deny even the smallest element of toleration to every section and creed within their bounds. But, however you put it, this particular block of land, this mass of human beings to be handed over, has never expressed the desire to go into the Nazi rule. I do not believe that even now—if their opinion could be asked, they would exercise such an option. . . .

I venture to think that in future the Czechoslovak State cannot be maintained as an independent entity. You will find that in a period of time which may be measured by years, but may be measured only by months, Czechoslovakia will be engulfed in the Nazi régime. Perhaps they may join it in despair or in revenge. At any rate, that story is over and told. But we cannot consider the abandonment and ruin of Czechoslovakia in the light only of what happened only last month. It is the most grievous consequence which we have yet experienced of what we have done and of what we have left undone in the last five years— five years of futile good intention, five years of eager search for the line of least resistance, five years of uninterrupted retreat of British power, five years of neglect of our air defences. Those are the features which I stand here to declare and which marked an improvident stewardship for which Great Britain and France have dearly to pay. We have been reduced in those five years from a position of security so overwhelming and so unchallengeable that we never cared to think about it. We have been reduced from a position where the very word "war" was considered one which would be used only by persons qualifying for a lunatic asylum. We have been reduced from a position of safety and power— power to do good, power to be generous to a beaten foe, power to make terms with Germany, power to give her proper redress for her grievances, power to stop her arming if we chose, power to take any step in strength or mercy or justice which we thought right—reduced in five years from a position safe and unchallenged to where we stand now. . . .

We are in the presence of a disaster of the first magnitude which has befallen Great Britain and France. Do not let us blind ourselves to that. It must now be accepted that all the countries of Central and Eastern Europe will make the best terms they can with the triumphant Nazi Power. The system of alliances in Central Europe upon which France has relied for her safety has been swept away, and I can see no means by which it can be reconstituted. The road down the Danube Valley to the Black Sea, the resources of corn and oil, the road which leads as far as Turkey, has been opened. In fact, if not in form, it seems to me that all those countries of Middle Europe, all those Danubian countries, will, one after another, be drawn into this vast system of power politics—not only power military politics but power economic politics—radiating from Berlin, and I believe this can be achieved quite smoothly and swiftly and will not necessarily entail the firing of a single shot. If you wish to survey the havoc of the foreign policy of Britain and France, look at what is happening and is recorded each day in the columns of the "Times.". . . .

[After quoting and summarizing news from Yugoslavia and Poland as typical:]

We are talking about countries which are a long way off and of which, as the Prime Minister might say, we know nothing. [*Interruption.*] The noble Lady says that that very harmless allusion is—

VISCOUNTESS ASTOR: Rude.

MR. CHURCHILL: She must very recently have been receiving her finishing course in manners. What will be the position, I want to know, of France and England this year and the year afterwards? What will be the position of that Western front of which we are in full authority the guarantors? The German army at the present time is more numerous than that of France, though not nearly so matured or perfected. Next year it will grow much larger, and its maturity will be more complete. Relieved from all anxiety in the East, and having secured resources which will greatly diminish, if not entirely remove, the deterrent of a naval blockade, the rulers of Nazi Germany will have a free choice open to them in what direction they will turn their eyes. If the Nazi dictator should choose to look westward, as he may, bitterly will France and England regret the loss of that fine army of ancient Bohemia which was estimated last week to require not fewer than 30 German divisions for its destruction.

Can we blind ourselves to the great change which has taken place in the military situation, and to the dangers we have to meet? . . .

This is only the beginning of the reckoning. This is only the first sip, the first foretaste of a bitter cup which will be proffered to us year by year unless by a supreme recovery of moral health and martial vigour, we arise again and take our stand for freedom as in the olden time.

PRIME MINISTER CHAMBERLAIN,
HOUSE OF COMMONS,
OCTOBER 5, 1938.

[Concluding the debate which began October 3, Chamberlain pleaded once again for peace:]

As regards future policy, it seems to me that there are really only two possible alternatives. One of them is to base yourself upon the view that any sort of friendly relations, or possible relations, shall I say, with totalitarian States are impossible, that the assurances which have been given to me personally are worthless, that they have sinister designs and that they are bent upon the domination of Europe and the gradual destruction of democracies. Of course, on that hypothesis, war has got to come, and that is the view—a perfectly intelligible view —of a certain number of hon. and right hon. Gentlemen in this House. . . .

If that is hon. Members' conviction, there is no future hope for civilisation or for any of the things that make life worth living. Does the experience of the Great War and of the years that followed it give us reasonable hope that if some new war started that would end war any more than the last one did? No. I do not believe that war is inevitable. Someone put into my hand a remark made by the great Pitt about 1787, when he said:

To suppose that any nation can be unalterably the enemy of another is weak and childish and has its foundations neither in the experience of nations not in the history of man.

It seems to me that the strongest argument against the inevitability of war is to be found in something that everyone has recognised or that has been recognised in every part of the House. That is the universal aversion from war of the people, their hatred of the notion of starting to kill one another again. . . .

What is the alternative to this bleak and barren policy of the inevitability of war? In my view it is that we should seek by all means in our power to avoid war, by analysing possible causes, by trying to remove them, by discussion in a spirit of collaboration and good will. I cannot believe that such a programme would be rejected by the people of this country, even if it does mean the establishment of personal contact with dictators, and of talks man to man on the basis that each, while maintaining his own ideas of the internal government of his country, is willing to allow that other systems may suit better other peoples. The party opposite surely have the same idea in mind even if they put it in a different way. They want a world conference. Well, I have had some experience of conferences, and one thing I do feel certain of is that it is better to have no conference at all than a conference which is a failure. The corollary to that is that before you enter a conference you must have laid out very clearly the lines on which you are going to proceed, if you are at least to have in front of you a reasonable prospect that you may obtain success. I am not saying that a conference would not have its place in due course. But I say it is no use to call a conference of the world, including these totalitarian Powers, until you are sure that they are going to attend, and not only that they are going to attend, but that they are going to attend with the intention of aiding you in the policy on which you have set your heart.

I am told that the policy which I have tried to describe is inconsistent with the continuance, and much more inconsistent with the acceleration of our present programme of arms. I am asked how I can reconcile an appeal to the country to support the continuance of this programme with the words which I used when I came back from Munich the other day and spoke of my belief that we might have peace for our time. I hope hon. Members will not be disposed to read into words used in a moment of some emotion, after a long and exhausting day, after I had driven through miles of excited, enthusiastic, cheering people—I hope they will not read into those words more than they were intended to convey.

I do indeed believe that we may yet secure peace for our time, but I never meant to suggest that we should do that by disarmament, until we can induce others to disarm too. Our past experience has shown us only too clearly that weakness in armed strength means weakness in diplomacy, and if we want to secure a lasting peace, I realise that diplomacy cannot be effective unless the consciousness exists, not here alone, but elsewhere, that behind the diplomacy is the strength to give effect to it. . . .

I cannot help feeling that if, after all, war had come upon us, the people of this country would have lost their spiritual faith altogether. As it turned out the other way, I think we have all seen something like a new spiritual revival, and I know that everywhere there is a strong desire among the people to record their readiness to serve their country, whereever or however their services could be most useful. I would like to take advantage of that strong feeling if it is possible, and although I must frankly say that at this moment I do not myself clearly see my way to any particular scheme, yet I want also to say that I am ready to consider any suggestion that may be made to me, in a very sympathetic spirit.

Finally, I would like to repeat what my right hon. Friend the Chancellor of the Exchequer said yesterday in his great speech. Our policy of appeasement does not mean that we are going to seek new friends at the expense of old ones, or, indeed, at the expense of any other nations at all. I do not think that at any time there has been a more complete identity of views between the French Government and ourselves than there is at the present time. Their objective is the same as ours —to obtain the collaboration of all nations, not excluding the totalitarian States, in building up a lasting peace for Europe. That seems to me to be a policy which would answer my hon. Friends' appeal, a policy which should command the support of all who believe in the power of human will to control human destiny. If we cannot here this afternoon emulate the patriotic unanimity of the French Chamber, this House can by a decisive majority show its approval of the Government's determination to pursue it.

[The vote which followed supported the government 369 to 150.]

Georges Bonnet

IN DEFENSE OF FRENCH POLICY

Georges Bonnet, Foreign Minister of France, shares with Neville Chamberlain the major blame for the Munich settlement in the eyes of the critics. Before he became foreign minister in April 1938 he had held various posts in French cabinets from 1925, and had represented France at the League of Nations and as ambassador to the United States. Although his memoirs, from which the excerpts below are taken, were not published until 1946, after the hopes of peace under the Munich Agreement had been dissipated by the outbreak of war, his explanation of French policy properly belongs with the contemporary views of the crisis. Upon what does he base his defense of French policy? Does he differ from Chamberlain and Hoare in his attitude toward the crisis?

AT the time when in Germany work shifts took turns night and day in order to fabricate tanks and airplanes, when fortifications at the frontier were being feverishly completed by five hundred thousand mobilized men, when a million and a half soldiers were already in barracks or on maneuvers, what was France doing?

France was on vacation! A chronicler reports the fact with enthusiasm in the press: "In the Parisian region alone, 500,000 persons have left, 300 supplementary trains have assured their departure. . . . The spectacle at the capital is repeated in all the railway stations of the great cities. But on the roads also the cars, motorcycles, and everything that rolls increase. They leave. They have gone." Oh, yes! they have left, some for the beaches, others for the fields, still others for the mountains. Everyone rests! The paid holidays were to last fifteen days. But by a crafty cumulation of legal holidays, factories closed their doors 23 days during the month of August, which was thus almost entirely lost for national production. And strikes succeeded in reducing to nothing the economic activity of the country. . . .

Daladier, head of the government and minister of war, was better placed than anyone to understand the tragic character of the situation. On August 21 he addressed the country by radio. He explained Germany's effort. He renewed the assurance that the franc would not be devalued. He affirmed that it was necessary to modify the forty-hour law . . . . The speech was clear and courageous; it did not seem to offer grounds for criticism. Moreover it conformed with the conclusions of the commission of inquiry concerning production, and observed absolute moderation. It nevertheless aroused a heated controversy and opened a grave political crisis.

* * *

What were, then, the singular illusions of our compatriots and in particular of those who opposed the measures wanted by the president of the council, in demanding that he stand up to Germany? Admitting for a moment a hypothesis which was dear to them: that of the "Hitlerian bluff," should we stop taking energetic measures in response to German dispositions? An objective observer would then rightly ask which side was bluffing, and who were the ones who on

From Georges Bonnet, *Défense de la paix:* Vol. I. *De Washington au Quai d'Orsay* (Geneva: Constant Bourguin, 1946), pp. 177–180, 196–200, 202–203, 219–229, 247–251, 267–271, 275–278, 281–287. Translated by the editor.

the morrow would be ready to put their menaces into effect: the Germans who were working and exerting themselves night and day in the factories and the barracks, or the others who lounged on the beaches or in the mountains?

Everything therefore complicated the task of the French government. . . . The minister of foreign affairs could but ponder the last phrases of the report of August 18 from the French ambassador at Berlin: "The Third Reich continues night and day to develop its fortifications and its military preparations, and acts in every way like a country which expects to face *a European war in the near future.*"

* * *

It was evident that there was not a minute to lose. On August 23 we learned in effect that the German ministers at Bucharest and Belgrade had made the following verbal communications to the Roumanian and Yugoslav governments:

The German government considers that it would find itself obliged to intervene if the Sudeten question was not settled rapidly and in a manner conformable in all points with the views of the German minority. In case France, in consequence of that intervention, should believe that it was obliged to act militarily against the Reich, the German government deems that France should be considered as having committed an act of aggression against Germany. . . .

The German *démarche* accompanied by a clearly expressed menace confirmed my opinion that the attack against Czechoslovakia had already been decided upon and that it would take place sometime in September.

I summoned M. Souritz, ambassador of the U.S.S.R. at Paris, on August 26 to inform him of the German maneuvers in Bucharest and Belgrade. Then I took up with him an examination of the general situation. I stated precisely that, up to that time and in spite of all our pressure, the governments of Roumania and Poland had refused to permit Russian troops to cross, or Russian planes to fly over, their territory. And I begged

him to ask his government if it had decided to disregard this double refusal, or at least to explain how it could practically bring its support to the Prague government.

At the same time I sent instructions to our ambassador in Moscow to pose the same question to Litvinov, people's commissar for foreign affairs. . . .

Since M. Coulondre was on vacation, it was M. Payart, plenipotentiary and *chargé d'affaires* for France, who took the prescribed step. As early as September 1, he saw the deputy commissar, Potemkin, who already knew of my interview with M. Souritz. M. Potemkin "still could not give any information of a nature to enlighten the French government." Besides, M. Payart was to see M. Litvinov himself on the morrow.

Actually, September 2, M. Litvinov received M. Payart. The latter immediately gave a telegraphic report of that important conversation, of which the essential passages follow:

I have repeated to M. Litvinov the question put by your telegram. The People's Commissar in the first place confirmed his previous declarations of principle according to which the U.S.S.R. had decided to fulfill by every possible means the obligations arising from its pact with Czechoslovakia, on condition that France observed its own. . . .

M. Litvinov once more indicated to me that given the negative attitude adopted by Warsaw and Bucharest, he saw *but one practical conclusion: that of recourse to the League of Nations. He mentioned, but to exclude it a priori, the eventuality of a forced passage of Soviet troops across Poland or Roumania without a decision of Geneva.* In his judgment every useful step should be taken in order to alert the League of Nations council immediately so that the Geneva machinery would be ready to be set in motion as soon as aggression occurred.

One sees that the position of the Soviet government had not been noticeably modified since the month of May. The consent of Roumania always remained the necessary condition for a military intervention of the U.S.S.R. But the Roumanian government now categorically made known its refusal.

I was to confirm this anew on September 11, 1938. We were at this time in full crisis over Czechoslovakia. The rupture between the Prague government and the Sudetens was thenceforth an accomplished fact. At Nuremberg, Hitler declaimed his threatening speech. All Europe was in agony. Despite everything, I resolved to travel to Geneva, where the annual session of the League assembly was about to open. The 11th of September I was at Geneva. I met first off M. Litvinov with whom, as in the preceding May, I had a long discussion of the decisions that the U.S.S.R. would be led to take in case of a German aggression against Czechoslovakia, if France itself made war on Germany in order to bring aid to the Prague government.

M. Litvinov confined himself exactly to the conversation of September 2 with M. Payart. The position of his government was immutable. It seemed to him indispensable to make an appeal to the council of the League of Nations and to obtain from it a recommendation to ask Roumania to let the Soviet troops and planes pass over its territory, lacking which any military action of the U.S.S.R. remained impossible.

But he believed that such a notice could have some influence on the Roumanian government. Finally, it remained well understood that it was France itself, whatever the circumstances, who would first afford its military aid to the Prague government.

I called to M. Litvinov's attention how long and uncertain that procedure appeared to be. Could the council rule in time, that is to say before the collapse of Czechoslovakia? There were in the rules of the League of Nations many procedural contrivances permitting indefinite postponements. Could one be sure that certain members of the League would not use them? Would not someone then appeal from the Council to the Assembly?

Moreover, since the decisions of the council of the League of Nations had to be taken unanimously, it was almost certain that this would not be realized, and that the council, which was known through precedents to be extremely conservative, would refuse to make clearly the recommendation wanted by the U.S.S.R. in order to convince Roumania.

Finally—whatever may happen—the Roumanian government firmly decided to refuse the passage of Russian troops across its territory.

M. Litvinov repeated that Soviet troops would not cross the Roumanian frontiers in order to bring aid to Czechoslovakia *without the assent of the Roumanian government.*

Therefore it was necessary to make an appeal to the Roumanian government anew. . . .

[Bonnet summarizes his discussion with Comnen, Roumanian foreign minister, September 11.]

That was my conversation with M. Comnen. It was decisive: *In no case,* would Roumania, bound by its own public opinion and by its treaties with Poland and Yugoslavia, both hostile to Prague, let Russian troops cross its territory. If the U.S.S.R. sought to disregard this veto, Roumania would defend itself and would be supported by Poland. If Russia intervened, it would thus find itself automatically at war with Poland and Roumania. That hypothesis, however, was most highly improbable, since the people's commissar for foreign affairs had declared that the U.S.S.R. would abstain from any military action if it had not obtained the previous consent of Bucharest, France having itself given the example. And the declaration made at Geneva by M. Litvinov some time later did not modify that perfectly clear position.

* * *

England could give but one assurance, that if the security of France was in danger she would immediately be at its side. But in such a case, what aid could be expected from Great Britain on the ground and in the air? London would reply: "Two non-motorized divisions and one hundred and fifty planes for the first six months of the war.". . .

September 13, after the rupture between Prague and the Sudetens, the position of the British government remained unchanged: "All for France. No other obligation!"

Thus the French government, in power for four months, had tried to divert the current of hostility or of indifference which had swept people into disregarding the misfortunes of Czechoslovakia. But all its efforts had been in vain.

In that critical moment what were, then, the respective forces of Czechoslovakia and France, and what chance did they have of victoriously resisting a German attack?

The overwhelming reply was indirectly given us some months later by the events in Poland. The latter had at its disposal twice as many troops as Czechoslovakia; it was nevertheless defeated in fifteen days. After that it was no longer necessary to demonstrate that Czechoslovakia with its thirty-five divisions would not have held very long before the German army! And in 1941 powerful Russia was itself able to escape from encirclement only by the grace of its territorial immensity which offered it the possibilities of unlimited retirement.

But we did not need the lesson of these terrible experiences in order to measure, beginning with 1938, the risks of military operations conducted solely with the forces of Czechoslovakia and France. It suffices to recall the opinion on this point of the interested parties themselves. . . .

On September 21, in effect, the Czechoslovak general staff got in touch with the French general staff. They noted that since the *Anschluss* the greater part of the fortifications established by their care, opposite Germany, had now been turned. If the Czechoslovak army tried to hold there, the German army could make a decisive and rapid strategical operation against them. Under these conditions, the Czechoslovak general staff thought that the defense of its territory should be established very much to the rear of these fortifications. The French general staff approved that concept from the technical point of view. It asked the ministry of foreign affairs only "if it could make known its opinion without diplomatic drawbacks." And our reply was affirmative.

Thus, if the war broke out, Czechoslovakia would be "immediately and completely submerged," according to the official English expression. Its aviation fields, its fortifications, its principal cities, its railway junctions would fall into the hands of the Germans. All that could be hoped for was a heroic resistance of the Czech army in the mountains of Bohemia. But we were all in agreement that the resistance could last for only a very short time.

What role could the French army play? To that question I myself was in a position to respond only indirectly. The minister of foreign affairs, in effect, was not a member of the higher council of war, nor of the navy, nor of the air force. He did not know the state of the army nor even the agreements of the general staff more fully than what they wished to reveal to him: The general staff had never agreed that military conventions with foreign countries could be discussed in the presence of Quai d'Orsay representatives!

[At a meeting of the permanent committee of national defense held in March 1938 under the second Léon Blum government, the minutes of which, Bonnet learned in August:]

Generalissimo Gamelin had recalled "that Russia did not border upon Germany; that the transportation of a Russian army by the only and the bad Roumanian railway was not to be envisaged." He had indicated that the eventual mobilization of Russia might make Poland and Roumania enter into action, but in a contrary sense. "The efficacy of Russian aid was conditioned by the attitude of Poland and Roumania."

On his side, General Vuillemin had said: "From the aerial point of view Russian intervention on behalf of Czechoslovakia is very difficult. Above all it would be necessary to fly over Poland and Roumania, which implies that they have taken a position. Moreover, there exist in Czechoslovakia very few fields —about forty—that German aviation would quickly render unusable." Russian aviation, whose bases were at that time far distant from Czechoslovakia, would find it practically impossible to land and its action would thus turn out to be paralyzed. The events of the Polish campaign of 1939 and later that of the aerial war in 1944–1945 were to demonstrate the exactness of these forecasts. . . .

But the minutes of the committee contained another passage of considerable interest, which concerned the state of French aviation. In response to a question put to him, General Vuillemin had replied: "If we have war with Germany, *in fifteen days French aviation will be destroyed.*" And Marshal Pétain, who was present, added: "In aviation it is as much the potential for construction as the initial force that counts; but this potential we do not have."

Some months later, under the ministry of Daladier, General Vuillemin went to Berlin to return the visit of the minister of air, General Milch, which he had made to Paris in 1937. It was then toward the middle of August 1938 and the German-Czechoslovak tension was becoming more and more sharp. On his return to Paris, General Vuillemin came to see me as was his wont after a trip abroad. . . .

This trip . . . had not relieved the general of the worries he had expressed to the permanent committee of national defense some time before. He reported to me:

Alas, If there is a war, in fifteen days the French air force would be destroyed. We have at our disposal only old planes whose speed is not above 300 or 350 kilometers an hour. Our air force is therefore completely outclassed by the German, which certainly has an average speed of 500 an hour, namely 200 kilometers more than ours. If war broke out, and if I had to take to the air with those antiquated planes, I would be obliged to have them flown by my most mediocre pilots, because they would, alas, be certainly sacrificed. I would have to keep the good aviators for the distant time when we would have modern planes and when we could fight the enemy with equal arms.

In saying these words, General Vuillemin, glorious soldier of the war of 1914

–1918 who had only just taken over the duties of chief of the air general staff, did not hide his emotion. He had to give with as much frankness the same warnings to his immediate chiefs, Daladier, minister of national defense, and Guy La Chambre, minister of the air.

As for the concerns of the land forces, of which Daladier was the supreme chief, I contented myself with the general views which he could afford me on the condition of the army and which sufficed to orient the foreign policy of the government. . . .

Meanwhile, some time before Munich, I also knew that Daladier had said to François-Poncet, returning to his post at Berlin: "We still need six months in order to equip our army with modern batteries capable of opposing the German artillery." And the cannon 90 for defense against airplanes was to begin to emerge only in the course of the second half of 1939.

An inferiority so deplorable existed essentially because Germany had begun its land rearmament in 1934, *two years* before France. . . .

Such were the dramatic and secret difficulties in the midst of which we struggled at the time when we were speaking high and mightily to Germany. They would not permit us to hope for a quick and certain victory. As Daladier has written since: ". . . one could not ask France alone to declare war upon Germany, alone to confront its armies and air force; and if she had done so, she would not have prevented Czechoslovakia from being submerged and having its cities destroyed in a few days."

Great Britain was in a deplorable military situation. Its army was almost nonexistent. Its effectives amounted to about 230,000 men, including the reserves of the regular army and the supporting services! Also we have seen that it could put at the disposition of France for the first six months of the war only about 30,000 combatants.

England had at its disposal only some hundreds of modern planes, incapable of holding their own against German squadrons ten times stronger. And its industry had just begun to manufacture 150 planes a month.

All this had been thoroughly summarized in the report which General Lelong, our military attaché at London, remitted to M. Corbin, November 8, a month after Munich.

He wrote: "At the time of the Munich crisis on what could we count? The balance-sheet could be put this way: The immediate British contribution in the air and on the ground is infinitesimal (two divisions of infantry—120 planes). Little hope, before some long months, of having a serious reinforcement of ground troops."

It was during September 1938 that I learned from Sir Eric Phipps in what an embryonic state British aviation was. Seeing my astonishment at the ridiculous number of planes put at our disposition by England in case of war, the ambassador said to me: "Alas, we cannot do better!" And he gave me the most precise and complete explanations with great frankness. This reciprocal confidence was indispensable between allies. It was moreover the result of the accords of London of April 28 and 29, which envisaged a sincere and complete exchange of military information between us. . . .

If the English air force was almost nonexistent in October 1938 its navy was still far from having completed its program. The big warships which had been laid down would be ready only in the course of the year 1940. "It could not render us any aid in the Mediterranean," as the report of General Lelong noted. And, what is more, the British admiralty was to ask us, in case of war, to send from the Mediterranean into the Atlantic one of our modern units, the *Dunkerque* or the *Strasbourg*, to aid the British navy in protecting our common convoys against German submarines.

That was the alarming state to which France and England were reduced by the disarmament that they had prolonged in good faith, fully believing that they were serving peace, right up to 1936.

[After describing the Berchtesgaden meeting and the Czechoslovak objections to a plebiscite, Bonnet tells the story of the Anglo-French meeting in London, September 18–19, and the proposal sent to Czechoslovakia to make territorial cessions to Germany. On the evening of the 20th the French ambassador in Prague, de Lacroix, telegraphed a rumor that the answer would be negative or designed to gain time.]

Finally, at 9:15 P.M., September 20, we received a second telegram from M. de Lacroix. He had been summoned along with his British colleague by M. Krofta, Czechoslovak minister of foreign affairs, who had handed them the counter-proposal of the Czechoslovak government. The latter invoked the breadth of the concessions which the government had made in the end to the Sudetens, and even the acknowledgment by record of the latter. The government refused a solution decided upon outside itself, and proposed recourse to arbitration on the basis of the German-Czechoslovak treaty of October 16, 1926. It concluded "by making an appeal to France and Great Britain asking them to reconsider the question."

But while I was reading the telegram about 9:30 P.M., I was called to the phone by M. de Lacroix who was devotedly at his post night and day. He told me: "I have just transmitted to you a reply of the Czechoslovak government demanding the application of the treaty of arbitration. Do not consider it as definitive. *The president of the Czechoslovak council has just called me to make a new proposal,* very important, of which I informed you by a telegram that you will receive immediately."

I informed Daladier and begged him to come to meet me at the Quai where I awaited the second message. I asked the cipher service to give priority to the telegram from Prague and to bring it to me without losing a second as they deciphered it. After a short wait it was finally on my table. *It had come at 9:50 P.M. It was quite different from the preceding telegram received at 9:30 P.M. which announced the decision of the Czechoslovak government to have recourse to arbitration.* Between the reception of the one and the other, only twenty minutes had elapsed. What had happened? How to explain the about-face?

I read attentively this text which is of such capital importance that I transcribe it here completely. Here is what M. Lacroix wrote me:

The president of the council has just summoned me. In accord, he tells me, with the president of the Republic, he declares that if I come that same night and declare to M. Beneš that in case of war between Germany and Czechoslovakia on account of the Sudeten Germans, France, because of its engagements with England, would not march, the president of the Republic would take note of that declaration; the premier would immediately convoke the cabinet, of which all the members are at present in agreement with the president of the Republic and with himself to yield . . .

The Czechoslovak rulers need that cover in order to accept the Franco-English proposal. They are sure of the army, whose chiefs have declared that a conflict alone with Germany would be suicide. M. Hodža says that the *démarche* which he suggests is the only means of saving the peace.

He wants everything finished before midnight if possible or in any case in the course of the night. The premier will make the same communication to the minister of England.

What was the reason for that apparent about-face?

It is certain that the Czechoslovak government did not want to seem to be making of its own accord concessions at Berlin which its opinion judged excessive. It therefore took an official attitude consisting of a demand for the application of the treaty of arbitration with Germany.

But at the same time it did not ignore the extreme gravity of the situation that the heads of the army when consulted had themselves recognized: It was a question of avoiding the "suicide of Czechoslovakia!" It was therefore ready in reality to accept a compromise; but the trick consisted in asking France and England secretly to put pressure upon them which would justify in the eyes of their public opinion the acceptance of the Franco-English plan and would leave us with all the responsibility.

Some moments later, Daladier arrived at the Quai d'Orsay and came to my office where also were M. Léger, general secretary of the ministry, and M. Jules Henry, director of my staff. We discussed the whole situation from 11:15 P.M. till 12:30 A.M. We learned that the response of Great Britain to Prague would be affirmative. We thought that we could not refuse the Czechoslovak government the "cover" which it needed for its reputation.

But I insisted vehemently that Daladier call together the ministerial council: The members of the government, apprized of the present situation, could but approve our proposals and we would thus avoid subsequent criticism. Daladier shared my opinion, but he drew to my attention the physical impossibility of convening the council: The president of the Republic was at Rambouillet, many ministers were absent from Paris. How much time would it take to bring together the others? On the other hand, the reply had to be given very quickly, and if possible before midnight; now it was past eleven o'clock. Actually, in the course of our discussion, I was called to the phone twice from Prague, whence I was asked if the French reply was ready "because the Czechoslovak government was awaiting it impatiently!"

After a discussion we decided that it was advisable to send M. de Lacroix instructions detailed enough to orient the conversation he had to have with M. Hodža. Daladier, Léger, Jules Henry, and I began to draft it. Each phrase was discussed and corrected; finally our instructions were ready. They emphasized that "the procedure envisaged by France and Great Britain appeared, in the present circumstances, as the only means of preventing German entry into Czechoslovakia." If the Czechoslovak government rejected the plan which had been submitted to it there would then be war with Germany. But England, in such a case, would certainly not be associated with France in order to exert a joint military action. Now, "without England,

French aid to Czechoslovakia would be ineffective." *Of the truth of that the Czechoslovak government had been advised many times and notably on the 16th of July.*

Meanwhile before telephoning this message to Prague, we judged it necessary, the premier and I, to inform the president of the Republic. I myself called M. Albert Lebrun at Rambouillet by direct line. I insisted, despite the late hour and the president himself answered me. I explained the situation to him and read to him line by line the telegram received from Prague and the reply which we had just prepared with the premier. The president of the Republic gave his agreement, while regretting, like us, that we were obliged to take decisions so precipitously.

Despite all our haste and all our good will, time had passed. It was half past twelve when we made known our instructions to M. de Lacroix. It was understood that he would be inspired by them in the conversations he was to have with M. Hodža, to whom he replied verbally.

An hour later, the British government let us know the terms of a telegram it had sent to its minister in Prague. It thought that the Anglo-French proposals constituted the only chance of preventing an immediate German attack. If Prague maintained its application for recourse to the German-Czechoslovak treaty of arbitration, a second visit of the Prime Minister to M. Hitler would have no result. The English government therefore begged the Czechoslovak government "to reflect at once and seriously before events occurred for which it [i.e., the English government] could not accept the least responsibility."

Toward two o'clock in the morning, the French and English ministers carried to the Czechoslovak government the reply requested. The latter met immediately afterward as a council of ministers. The deliberations lasted until six o'clock in the morning. But, contrary to our expectations, no telegram from Prague arrived immediately. And it was only at half past twelve that M. de Lacroix telephoned to inform me of the situation. The Czechoslovak government was no longer in the same state of mind as the night before: As a result of information received by telephone during the night, it could believe that the French government would be obliged to modify its position under the pressure of parliamentary opinion and would even be led to resign! Under these conditions, it wanted to wait some hours before giving a definitive reply. It would demand without doubt that our communication of the previous night be remitted in writing, as the minister of England had done. I agreed upon this point, but recalled that our reply had been made only in consequence of M. Hodža's appeal to M. de Lacroix.

Early in the afternoon, Sir Eric Phipps telephoned me personally. He told me that the British government was greatly disturbed by the silence of Prague, which only the night before was pressing the French and English governments to reply before midnight. Why that hurry if it was not to make a decision immediately? This delay was incomprehensible. It might be owing to the rumor spread in the Czechoslovak capital of the possible resignation of the French government. Sir Eric Phipps concluded by saying that it was out of the question for London to modify its attitude. And if it were necessary, Mr. Newton would make a new *démarche* to affirm it once again to M. Beneš and M. Hodža.

But that intervention was not necessary. At 5 o'clock M. Krofta, Czechoslovak minister of foreign affairs, called in the ministers of France and England to announce to them that the Czechoslovak government was ready to accept the Anglo-French plan. Mr. Neville Chamberlain, who had thus far been prevented, prepared to leave for Godesberg.

There, supported by the documents, is the objective account of the dramatic events of those days of September 20 and 21, just as they developed.

* * *

[After summarizing the meeting at Godesberg and the military measures taken by France and Czechoslovakia on September 23–24, Bonnet turns to the Anglo-French meeting in London, September 25–26.]

Before again departing with me for London, Daladier summoned the council of ministers on Sunday, September 25, early in the afternoon. We commented for him in broad outline on the German memorandum which had been transmitted to us. We judged it impossible to recommend to the Czechoslovak government its adoption; the plebiscite demanded by Hitler in some regions where, according to all indications, the density of the Czech population was well above that of the German population seemed to us particularly excessive. The mobilization of part of the French army and the Czechoslovak general mobilization demonstrated our will not to give way before unacceptable arbitrary demands. Despite the extreme tension we persevered right up to the end in our effort to maintain the peace. At the close of the council a communiqué recorded *the unanimous agreement of the government to approve the declarations that the premier and the minister of foreign affairs proposed to take to London to the British government.* . . .

In the evening, at 9 o'clock, we were again at 10 Downing Street. The British ministers, members of the limited cabinet, awaited us. Beside Mr. Neville Chamberlain there were Lord Halifax, Sir John Simon, and Sir Samuel Hoare, and, near by, Sir Horace Wilson, intimate councilor of the prime minister, Lord Robert Vansittart and Sir Alexander Cadogan.

At the opening of the meeting, Mr. Chamberlain told us, as always, with great pains to be objective and exact, the ups and downs of the interview that he had had with Chancellor Hitler. He concluded that he had simply undertaken to send the memorandum for decision to the Czechoslovak government and to report to the French government. He asked us our impression, which we expressed without any difficulty. We considered the new claims set forth by Hitler in his memorandum of Godesberg to be

unacceptable and we could not recommend them to Czechoslovakia, which had decided to reject them.

"And if Germany, in consequence of this refusal, invades Czechoslovakia?" asked the Prime Minister.

In that case France will immediately accord her assistance to Czechoslovakia.

Daladier next asked the Prime Minister if one could not immediately send to its appointed place the international commission envisaged since our discussions of September 18. Mr. Neville Chamberlain replied that that solution did not have a chance of being accepted by Germany.

After that group of very short observations, the diplomatic part of the conference ended. The French and British governments were agreed in rejecting all of the demands contained in the Godesberg memorandum.

Then a new and long discussion took place which bore entirely on military problems. Mr. Neville Chamberlain, Sir Samuel Hoare, and Sir John Simon put to Daladier a series of questions. What means did the French army have at its disposition to "assist" Czechoslovakia? What was our plan of battle against Germany? Could France put on foot a sufficient number of infantry divisions backed by a powerful air force, equipped with modern arms, to mount an offensive which would overthrow Germany?

Daladier, minister of national defense and of war, was on the carpet! He replied energetically. He obviously did not want to give precise details which would run the risk of discouraging his inquisitors too much. The latter continued tenaciously and repeated their questioning on the same point: "Czechoslovakia, we are certain of it, will be overthrown in a few days at least. France would then face Germany alone. What means will be at your disposal to conquer it?" Daladier began his explanation again and the meeting continued without progress.

The Prime Minister intervened. He told us that he had received the most disquieting information on the state of French aviation and on the incapacity of our factories to replace machines lost in the early days of the war. If a rain of bombs fell immediately on Paris, on the air fields, on the stations, on rail centers, would France be able to defend itself and to counterattack?

Daladier refused to commit himself further on the technical matter, and retaliated by himself asking Mr. Neville Chamberlain: "Do you yourself accept Hitler's plan?"

"It is not for me," replied Mr. Chamberlain. "It is up to the Czechoslovak government to express its opinion on this point."

"But then," replied M. Daladier, "do you think that France ought to remain passive?"

"It is not for the British government to express an opinion on what France should do, but rather the French government!"

The discussions thus dragged on without conclusion for a part of the night, always on the military matter, so much so that neither Lord Halifax nor I myself took part in it.

The British Prime Minister finally asked if it were not possible to have General Gamelin come to London, and as we were all in agreement on this point, they telephoned to the general begging him to be in London early the following morning.

Toward three o'clock in the morning after these long and distressing debates, we left 10 Downing Street where awaited us in front of the door a crowd of curious people, journalists, and photographers, and we returned to the embassy. I found on my table several important telegrams.

One was from M. de Lacroix, who told us of the conversation which he had just had with M. Beneš.

"The president of the Republic summoned me," he wrote, "this morning at 8 o'clock. He had become acquainted during the night with the German memorandum and the map annexed to it. He was in a high state of emotion. From his indignation, which was expressed in jerky phrases, I extract the following points: M. Beneš is acquainted with the difficulties of France. He does not want to increase the difficulties either for France or for England. He maintains with his government acceptance of the Anglo-French proposal remitted last Monday [September 19]. But he cannot go farther. He will not go farther. The plebiscite is unacceptable to him. It is a means of disorganizing the state. It would give cause for the gravest trouble; blood would be spilled."

M. Beneš in conclusion asked that the French government declare at London that France would not allow this plan. It was the same position as we had just been taking and which had been noted by the British government.

After this first telegram I opened a second. It came from the French minister of the interior and stated that there were no gas masks to distribute to the Parisian population! He asked that we do our utmost to procure a million in London. Of course London would reply on the morrow that they themselves had not a sufficient quantity for the London population, and that they could not furnish any to us. These two telegrams seemed to illustrate the debate between Daladier and the English ministers pursued during the night. It was evident that, in that crisis, our ends far surpassed our means!

The following morning we returned to Downing Street accompanied by our collaborators and by General Gamelin, who had just arrived. There was in the first place a short meeting among Daladier and General-in-Chief Gamelin, Mr. Chamberlain, Sir Thomas Inskip, British minister of defense coordination, and General Viscount Gort. It was devoted entirely to the most technical military questions.

I therefore did not participate, nor did Lord Halifax. This permitted me to make a quick acquaintance, along with M. Léger and my assistants, of the latest dispatches. Lord Halifax, on his side, prepared himself for the diplomatic conference which began twenty minutes later with the same delegates as the preceding night. The Prime Minister said to us that he understood perfectly the French position. He nevertheless wanted to make a supreme effort to maintain the peace. He was therefore sending to Berchtesgaden his assistant Sir Horace Wilson as bearer of a personal letter in which he stated that the German proposals had been rejected by the Czechoslovak government. He invited Hitler to agree to negotiate rather than to resort to force. Then he made known to us in writing the terms in which he had expressed our declaration:

"The French government has made known to us that it would completely fulfill its obligations in case of a German attack on Czechoslovakia." And Mr. Chamberlain added: "In case that France, in executing its obligations devolving from the treaties, were involved in hostilities against Germany, the United Kingdom would feel obliged to come to its aid."

One sees that the letter of the Prime Minister defined without equivocation the position of France, resolved to give its assistance against every aggression. As for England, the formula employed by Mr. Neville Chamberlain, even though it did not signify, one will observe, that England was resolved to enter war immediately against Germany on the side of France, was nevertheless firmer than that which the British government had employed up to that time.

* * *

[After recounting the failure of the Wilson mission to Hitler and Roosevelt's appeal to Hitler and Czechoslovakia to seek a peaceful solution to their crisis, he continued with the events of September 27.]

It was the day when an important council of ministers met at the Elysée. In advance I had a long conversation with the president of the council. The dispatches of the night were always very alarming. However, we did not consider deciding at that moment upon general mobilization. That was one of the most serious steps which, because of our engagements with London, presupposed a previous consultation with the British government. It was thought, on the other hand, that there was an advantage, from the military point of view, in achieving the mobilization of specialists and young elements of the army before summoning to the barracks all mobilizable Frenchmen, whose services to the army could not be immediately employed and whose

absence would paralyze the economic life of the country.

On the contrary, if our peaceable efforts failed and if Germany mobilized or attacked Czechoslovakia, the French government, as it had the right to do, would decree general mobilization. But it would convoke parliament at once in order to demand from it a vote of confidence; this vote was required before sending an ultimatum to Germany, by virtue of the arrangements of the 1875 constitution.

In consequence, we agreed with Daladier to make the following proposals to the council: to extend our mobilization measures by calling to the colors more new classes which would bring to two million men our mobilized effectives. It remained understood that if Czechoslovakia was the object of a German aggression, France would fulfill towards it its duty of aid, with the approval of parliament. But we pursued our efforts to avoid finding ourselves alone at war with Germany and to obtain a peaceable settlement in the terms of the Franco-English plan of September 18.

The government which then met at the Elysée approved our decisions after a confused debate. It was understood that the military problems, should the occasion arise, would be raised before the permanent committee of national defense.

While the council of ministers was ending at Paris, Sir Horace Wilson met Hitler again on the 27th at noon. He announced to him that he would depart for London and asked him if he had a message to give to Mr. Neville Chamberlain. "None," replied Hitler, "except that Prague has a choice of two solutions: Either forthrightly accept the German memorandum or reject it. If they reject it, this will be war. I will smash the Czechs. Prague will be bombarded. The Czech army will be put to route and Doctor Beneš will be forced to flee ignominiously."

The menace was direct and harsh; the retort had been fixed in advance with us at London by the British Prime Minister. Sir Horace Wilson had reserved it for that critical moment. Here is the scene as told us by Sir Nevile Henderson, who was present at the interview:

When it was clear that Hitler's determination to go to war was quite inflexible, Sir H. Wilson said that he was charged by the Prime Minister to give him a message to the following effect: "If, in pursuit of her treaty obligations, France became actively engaged in hostilities against Germany, the United Kingdom would feel obliged to support her." Hitler's answer was that he could only take note of this communication. It meant, he said, that if France elected to attack Germany, England felt obliged to attack Germany, also. Sir H. Wilson attempted to refute this interpretation of his statement, but Hitler declined to be convinced. "If France and England strike," he shouted, "let them do so. It is a matter of complete indifference to me. I am prepared for every eventuality. I can only take note of the position. It is Tuesday today, and by next Monday we shall be at war." On this depressing note the interview ended. Sir Horace flew back to London early the same afternoon.

The same day Hitler sent a reply to Mr. Neville Chamberlain's letter. He reiterated the promise that he had made publicly at the Sports Palace and that he was to violate odiously on March 15, 1939:

There can, therefore, be not the slightest question whatsoever of a check to the independence of Czechoslovakia. It is, on the contrary, a well-known fact that Czechoslovakia after the cession of the Sudeten German territory would constitute a healthier and more unified economic organism than before.

But he affirmed that he was resolved to occupy the regions claimed on the date which he had fixed, no matter what the consequences might be.

*   *   *

In that historic night of the 27th and 28th of September 1938 most of us thought that war could no longer be avoided.

From Berlin, Ambassador Nevile Henderson wrote that "with faint hope I retired to bed on Tuesday night." And M. François-Poncet telegraphed that German general mobilization and the attack on Czechoslovakia were set for the 28th at 2 P.M.

On his part, at Paris, toward 11:30, the ambassador of England came to see me again for the fourth time in the course of the evening. He announced gravely that Germany would open hostilities on the morrow, the 28th, at the beginning of the afternoon. He added that his government was sending Hitler a last proposal authorizing, in accord with Prague, the immediate entry of German troops into an important part of the Sudeten territories. Would it be accepted? One remained uncertain.

At the ministry of foreign affairs everyone was staying up. Telegrams arrived without a break from all the capitals. Hardly deciphered, sometimes even while being deciphered, when they were important, they were brought immediately to my office. The court was full of cars, the vestibules, the reception rooms of the ground floor were illuminated as on festival nights; but anxiety reigned. A crowd of journalists, of parliamentarians come for news, surged about, but stopped at the sill of the double doors of my office where no one entered save my co-workers, and where I worked in peace.

*   *   *

In that night of watching and alarm one unanimous desire was manifested: that of peace. From all quarters they asked us to avoid the rupture of negotiations between Prague and Berlin. The most sensational intervention had been that of President Roosevelt, who had just proposed the immediate meeting of a conference of interested countries.

We decided to uphold and to utilize that initiative. I requested M. Corbin to go see Lord Halifax and to explore with him how the idea of President Roosevelt could be realized, by obtaining, according to his wish, the concurrence of the Italian government, which might have a decisive influence on Hitler. It was three o'clock in the morning that M. Corbin in London received my telegram thus drawn up: "Mr. Roosevelt has just proposed the calling of a conference in order to settle the Czechoslovak problem. France will associate itself with this initiative as will England. But it would be good for Italy likewise to support the proposal. I beg you to talk with Lord Halifax on this subject."

At the same time I sent instructions to our ambassador in Berlin to see Hitler very early the next morning. It will be remembered that the British government was going to submit to Berlin a compromise proposal allowing the immediate entry of German troops into a part of the Sudeten territories in the Eger region. The French government encouraged that proposal. It was prepared even to enlarge it. It was inclined to *propose* to Prague the evacuation by the first of October of some supplementary territories chosen among those indicated in the conversation held on September 18 between M. de Lacroix and the president of the Czechoslovak Republic, but it remained understood that the French government would not tolerate any act of violence.

Thus on September 28 at one A.M. I addressed to M. François-Poncet the telegram of which the following are the essential passages:

Paris, the 28th September at 1 A.M
FRENCH AMBASSADOR BERLIN
ABSOLUTE PRIORITY

According to the ambassador of England it is not only mobilization but the opening of hostilities that is envisaged for tomorrow at 2 P.M.

Sir Eric Phipps has just communicated to me a proposal that his government is submitting to Berlin and which includes the immediate entry of German troops into Egerland.

I beg you to ask your British colleague to let you know without delay if that proposal is accepted.

If not, and in order to attempt a last effort to avoid the irreparable, you should urgently submit to M. Hitler himself, in the name of the government, a proposal which, *repeating the conditions of execution of this last British suggestion,* would allow an immediate occupation of more important territory.

Then, after having geographically defined what that territory might be—which represented a part of the zones whose cession had been accepted by Prague according to the Franco-English plan of September 18—I added:

If the German government lets you know that it would be ready to accept this proposal, the French government would employ all its power to bring the Czechoslovak government around before the first of October. But this would evidently be impossible if military operations began tomorrow.

This outline is approximate and would have to be made precise, it being well understood that the fortifications would remain in the hands of the Czechs. . . .

Upon the arrival of this telegram, about five o'clock in the morning of the 28th, M. François-Poncet requested an audience with Hitler. At ten o'clock he had not yet been received by the chancellor. He wondered about it with Ambassador Sir Nevile Henderson, to whom he confided that he "feared the worst." Finally, after a long wait, at 11:15 the French ambassador was admitted to Hitler's presence.

M. François-Poncet laid before him the views of the French government. Prague would accept the immediate cession of certain Sudeten regions. For the rest, it was advisable to await the decision of the international commission whose creation was envisaged. In any case, Hitler should not make a mistake. If he proceeded further and if he attacked Czechoslovakia, France would give assistance to its ally. And that would be general war. "It is uniquely upon Hitler that the safeguarding of European peace depends."

Thus, at that decisive hour, in the presence of the German chancellor, the French ambassador maintained the position that I had defined in the name of the French government. France refused to tolerate a new aggression by Germany. The mobilization of two million Frenchmen attested that the warning to Hitler would be executed.

But the French government, giving satisfaction to the views of London and Washington, agreed to submit to Prague a diplomatic settlement of the Sudeten affair, which safeguarded the Czechoslovak fortifications.

The conversation between the French ambassador and Hitler lasted an hour. Ribbentrop, who was present, intervened in the discussion, but solely to place in evidence whatever was unfavorable to the Reich. In the middle of the conversation, about 11:40, Hitler quitted the room in order to receive the Italian Ambassador Attolico, who had just arrived bearing an urgent appeal from Mussolini asking Hitler to postpone general mobilization for twenty-four hours. Hitler soon returned to the French ambassador and continued the discussion with him for twenty minutes. Then, in taking M. François-Poncet to the door of his workroom, he said to him: "My only care is to withdraw the Sudeten Germans at the earliest from the heightened oppression that they have suffered for several days. Your government has made an effort at conciliation to which I cannot reply by a categorical refusal. I need to reflect more. I shall let you know my response very quickly."

M. Poncet returned to the French embassy and by telephone immediately recounted the conversation in the terms I have just recalled. One can divine with what emotion I listened to his recital: "Does Hitler maintain his order of general mobilization for today at 2 P.M.?" "I still know nothing about it," replied M. Poncet, "My impression is much more favorable."

Some minutes after M. Poncet's departure, Hitler received Sir Nevile Henderson, who came to him bearing a last personal communication from the British Prime Minister. Mr. Chamberlain, who had been put in touch with President Roosevelt in the course of the night in order to discuss with him the project of the conference forecast in his message, now let Hitler know that Germany could have satisfaction in its essential claims without recourse to war, and that he was even ready to discuss the question anew with him.

Hitler did not make an immediate response to Sir Nevile, and when the latter left the chancellor, about 1 P.M., he remained in doubt.

In reality the essential decision had already been taken by Hitler since 11:40 while M. François-Poncet was still at the chancellery. He had postponed general mobilization for twenty-four hours....

At two o'clock in the afternoon, M. François-Poncet phoned me to announce that Hitler had decided to delay the entry of German troops into Czechoslovakia and that he proposed the reunion of a conference which would be held at Munich on the morrow of the 28th of September and to which the heads of the French, Italian, and English governments would be invited. Thus was shoved into the distance the nightmare of war which had pursued us all that previous night of watching and of anguish! Daladier immediately accepted the invitation made to him.

The announcement of the conference provoked an immense outburst of enthusiasm in the whole world, notably in Great Britain, in America, and in France....

Thus, on that day of September 28, 1938, the joy of seeing war avoided bloomed in the hearts of the most sincere democrats.

I was informed at the end of the afternoon that the Italian and German foreign ministers would attend the conference at Munich. I was asked if I would accompany the head of the French government. I made known that I would prefer to remain in Paris and I asked M. Léger to replace me beside the head of the government. But I gave the secretary general, as was natural, a note precisely summarizing my point of view concerning the conference which was going to begin. I prepared a short memorandum, of which the outline was as follows: It was necessary to reach an accord, but in ceding to Germany only the territories where the predominance of the German population was evident, preserving certain industrial centers of Czechoslovakia, and in obtaining, for the new frontiers, the guarantee of the invited powers.

Yet one point seemed to me especially essential: It was not to restrict oneself to the solution of the Sudeten affair, but to profit from the grievous sacrifice demanded of the Czechoslovak government to establish a durable peace. We ought then to propose the enlargement of the meeting at Munich and to transform it into a general conference of all the powers: the United States, the U.S.S.R., Poland, the Balkan states, who would examine and settle all the litigious problems in Europe.

Thus, on the eve of the Munich meet-ing the French government did not at all envisage a precarious entente with Germany, made with Czechoslovakia as scapegoat. It hoped for a general accord established among *all* the countries of our continent, which would save Europe from ruin and chaos, fatal consequences of a new war.

Pertinax

BONNET: A GRAVEDIGGER OF FRANCE

Pertinax, pseudonym of André Géraud, was one of the leading journalists of France. He was foreign editor of the *Echo de Paris,* 1917–1938, and editor of the weekly *L'Europe Nouvelle,* 1938–1940. Upon the fall of France in 1940 he escaped to England and was deprived of French citizenship by the Vichy government. Coming to the United States later in 1940 he contributed articles to American periodicals and published his severe attack upon French statesmen in *The Gravediggers of France,* a book that provoked a reply in an anonymous pamphlet which labeled it "The Slander of a Nation." Slander or true indictment, the book represented the informed opinion of an anti-Munich Frenchman. Written before Bonnet published his defense, does the excerpt below cast doubt upon the wisdom, if not the veracity, of Bonnet's account? Did he blunder? Did he connive at the outcome of the Munich crisis?

To sum up, there was only one hope of staving off the conflict. France, England, and Russia in association—if they could get together quickly enough —might succeed in frightening Hitler, in making him participate in a European settlement. Whatever the viewpoint from which the issue was examined, this conclusion was inescapable: without prompt co-operation with England and Russia peace was a forlorn hope.

Such a courageous policy had to be followed up to the end, and no shilly-shallying could be indulged in if France was to weather the storm. It was one of the sorriest strokes of luck that Georges Bonnet, thanks to the hazards of ministerial bargaining, should have been the man singled out to implement it. He could give it no more than he had in him: an inborn taste for double-dealing, the resources and the weakness of duplicity. And even that must be qualified. His duplicity was divorced from all strong purposes. It sprang from fear; it was hesitant and groping.

In the months and years after our defeat Bonnet has never varied in the explanation of his purpose as Minister of Foreign Affairs, and therefore most people today believe that from the outset he wished to yield to the dictators and never dared seriously impede them. But the story of his diplomacy is far more complicated.

Unable as he was to make up his own mind and to keep steadfastly to his resolve, he most often carried on two games simultaneously, one above board and the other below it. Of course he never sincerely stood for resistance, but neither did he unflinchingly stand for submission. The *Yellow Book* published in December 1939 presents him to posterity in an almost irreproachable light, according to the tenets of French diplomatic tradition. By contrast, an unbroken succession of incidents, reported by the most reliable authorities, lays bare the undermining work which he pursued under cover of the official policy. He kept on wrecking or unsettling with one hand whatever he did with the other. . . .

Specifically, Bonnet cannot escape indictment on three counts:

First, he exercised all his ingenuity to destroy our alliances, the only brake we could apply to Hitler's progress.

At the very start of the Czechoslovak crisis in 1938 we must note the London Conference of April 27–29, when Daladier and Bonnet tried to reach an understanding with Downing Street on a joint line of action. It was by harping on the theme of France bound in "honor" to support her ally that the Premier pried Mr. Chamberlain loose from his leanings toward non-intervention, which he had actually repudiated in the House of Commons on March 24, but to which he had meanwhile largely reverted. "Yes, Honor!" the Prime Minister repeated sadly. Honor! The word rung in Bonnet's ears as he listened without batting an eye. A sorry joke when you think of what was to happen! On May 20 the conflict between the Sudeten Germans (with Hitler behind them) and the Prague Government broke out. A false alarm. Germany was still short of the mark in her preparations, and Sir Nevile Henderson, at Berlin, used threatening language which perhaps went further than his instructions—as weak men are apt to do. However, on September 12, at the Nürnberg Congress, Hitler thundered out that the Bohemian blood brothers had a right to return to their German fatherland. It was up to France to say that she supported Beneš.

Meanwhile Bonnet, to put the advocates of resistance out of countenance, eagerly explained to everybody the numerous reasons why we should not bestir ourselves. Our air force was in a bad way. The Siegfried Line had to be reckoned with: General Gamelin could not outflank it since M. Janson, Belgian Foreign Minister, had just refused to allow us eventual passage through his country. Poland's course was more ambiguous than ever: Colonel Beck had not even concealed that his country would mobilize against Russia if the Soviets made any gesture toward helping the Czechs, and we had not been able to win assurances of free transit for Russian matériel. Marshal Smigly Rydz asserted that he had no recollection of the promises we had secured from him in return for the September 6, 1936, Rambouillet agreement (regarding the rearmament of his country); he went so far as to say that if the partition of Czechoslovakia was in the offing, no one would be surprised at Poland seizing what was hers in the Teschen area. Russia, Bonnet added, wants war between the Western Powers and Germany, but she will be careful to take no part in it. He did not whisper a single word concerning either the conference on policy, or the meeting of the League Council, or the staff consultations suggested by Litvinoff (who in Geneva, on September 11, had urged action, in similar terms, on Bonnet and Lord de la Warr), or the arrival in Prague of a Red Army general assigned to reconnoiter airfields. As to England, our Minister stopped at nothing in his efforts to persuade the government that we could in no way rely on her. He was greatly helped in his treachery by the personal views of the British Ambassador, Sir Eric Phipps. One day Bonnet even dared tell some callers of an altogether disconcerting "British note." Later he was obliged to admit that it was no more than a summary, written by himself of a conversation with Phipps.

Bonnet sought to make use of Belgians, Poles, Russians, British, and Czechs, to plant the seeds of doubt in French minds, and afterward he thought to make use of the French to frighten the rulers in Prague.

He kept saying that Beneš and Hodža did not want to fight and, at the bottom of their hearts, hoped that by declaring our unwillingness to intervene, through a *non possumus* as to our treaty obligations, by ostensibly building under their very feet a bridge to capitulation, we French would enable them to keep face before their own people. Beneš and Hodža were resigned to losing the Sudetenland, he argued, but they felt helpless as long as their fellow citizens kept faith in French assistance. To help those two statesmen the best thing to do was to discourage those fellow citizens.

To bolster his argument, Bonnet produced a telegram from M. de Lacroix, our Minister to Prague, dated September 20. The truth was that Bonnet had convinced Hodža of France's resolve to keep aloof and that Hodža in turn had tried to convince Beneš of it. But, true to type, Bonnet had avoided recording in any note or other official document what he had, time and again, so emphatically said in conversation. Beneš wanted to force him to do so. Not because he was determined to avoid throwing his country into the war, but because of his fear that France might leave Czechoslovakia in the lurch. He insisted that France's default must not come stealthily but be made tangible for his whole nation. At the same time he calculated that insistence upon a written statement would arouse Bonnet's opponents in the Paris Cabinet. This explains what passed between Paris and Prague on September 20, including the telegram freely quoted by Bonnet, later, to exculpate himself. The Minister held off committing himself in any way except verbally. To nail him down to his responsibility, M. de Lacroix insisted upon Bonnet dictating at once over the telephone the political statement requested by Beneš. Only lately has it been made known that Bonnet had Mistler with him that evening.

Such was Bonnet's method of strengthening our treaty bonds at a critical juncture. One can easily figure what sort of dispatches the ambassadors of England (Eric Phipps, a little man frozen with fear at the very name of Hitler), Russia, Poland, the United States, Italy, and Germany sent home after visiting the Quai d'Orsay. Hitler could rest undisturbed. France would not fight.

The surprising thing is not that governments both friendly and hostile should have become convinced of Bonnet's weakness, but that it should have taken them so long and that, mindful especially of Daladier's utterances, they should still occasionally have believed France capable of action. How furious was Bonnet when, on September 27, four days after the Godesberg ultimatum and twenty-four hours after the second Anglo-French meeting in London, Daladier was able to read aloud in support of his own firmer policy Chamberlain's second message, which Sir Horace Wilson was handing Hitler on that very day: "If France, in the fulfillment of her obliga-

tions, is actively drawn into war, England will feel obliged to support her." At the cabinet meeting the two men clashed violently over this formula. Bonnet's rage increased during the evening, when he learned of the Foreign Office's communiqué: if France went to war, she would be assisted by England and Russia. Bonnet pretended it was a forgery. In the same breath he branded as a lie the Reuter dispatch stating that on September 28, at 2 P.M., the Reich would decree a general mobilization. Bonnet had set himself up as Hitler's beater, the man to rouse and drive the game. He did not wish our political alliances and associations to give the despot the least worry or the German leader's brutality to become apparent to the French before they had given way.

The second count in the indictment against the Minister is that he turned the Munich Conference into a boundless diplomatic disaster. His daily remarks, made in his private office at the Quai d'Orsay or at some dinner table, were passed on to Berlin by the German Ambassador, Count Welzeck. I have already pointed out that at this time Keitel and Brauchitsch did not deem it wise to go to war. But Bonnet, unaware, waved a red flag in front of the bull. It is quite likely that the bellicose declamations at Nürnberg were, in this sense, the creation of our own Foreign Minister.

Indeed, Chamberlain's trip to Berchtesgaden was planned on September 13, in an effort to stop the dangerous interchange between the dictator and this weakling, an interchange carried on through the intermediary of the German Ambassador. But the remedy, in the end, proved worse than the disease.

Thus was taken, unwillingly, the first step toward the surrender of the Sudetenland. The men who sponsored it, who brought in Chamberlain so as to sidetrack Bonnet, explain that Daladier, when he put Chamberlain on the move, did not contemplate that Hitler should benefit by any territorial change except through an international procedure designed to hold in check and regulate the German onrush. So much so that Hitler, to get rid of the international procedure, hurled his Godesberg ultimatum which Chamberlain (who proved to be a feeble negotiator) could not get the cabinet meeting of September 24 to accept. So much so that the clash seemed to draw nearer and nearer.

On the twenty-eighth, all the odds were that Czechoslovakia would be invaded that very evening or the next day. At 10 A.M. the untiringly reiterated British proposal for a conference whose ultimate purpose was, indeed, to make of the little republic a Switzerland or a Belgium propped up by international guarantees was repeated for the third or fourth time. Spurred on by the secretary-general, Daladier and Bonnet decided that François-Poncet, French Ambassador in Berlin, should at once renew that British proposal with a slight variation in form and substance. The fate of our country hung upon what was going to happen. French ministers must not, before posterity, place themselves in the position of having taken as final for themselves also the refusal meted out, not to a representative of France, but to Sir Nevile Henderson and, earlier, to Sir Horace Wilson and Chamberlain himself. Poncet did not appear to understand the object of this French overture, which to him looked like asking for a rebuff. But upon explicit instructions he went to the Chancellery. At quarter past eleven he was received in audience. Shortly afterward he telephoned: "What a surprise! The Führer talked to me in an altogether different tone from that he used with my British colleague. 'I cannot say no to your suggestion,' he told me. 'I will give you a written answer this afternoon!' " That answer, instead of the note which had been announced, was the invitation to Munich.

What, then, had happened? We have since learned the truth. Otto Abetz and another personal envoy, whose opinion carried more weight with Hitler than did that of Welzeck, had sent word from Paris that Daladier would not give in, that partial mobilization, ordered on the twenty-sixth, was actually in process, that the clockworks were already in motion, and that things were slipping toward war. Hitler was convinced and

yielded. Mussolini also intervened, but, above everything else, it had begun to dawn upon Hitler that perhaps Bonnet's voice did not predominate in French ministerial councils.

At Munich it fell to the Premier and to Alexis Léger, who accompanied him, to stand by the principle of a Czechoslovakia assured of an independent life and international protection within straitened boundaries. On paper they won two important concessions: a delegate from Prague would sit on the Berlin Committee of Ambassadors, which was to map out the new frontiers, and the strict ethnical rule that all populations of German race belonged to Germany might be departed from in order to safeguard Czechoslovakia's national defense and economic existence.

On September 29, while the stiff argument with Hitler and Mussolini continued late into the night, Bonnet, at his Quai d'Orsay office, grew impatient of this slow pace. He telephoned and had others telephone. His newpapers were standing by, ready to speak out. Caillaux was holding up an article which would be printed and arouse a storm if the delay lasted too long. The conference came to an end. The Munich protocols more or less agreed with our requirements. But when the moment came to enforce them, what had been won was jeopardized by the weakness of the British and French representatives on the Berlin Committee. . . .

Daladier's policy in the juncture is hard to defend. He really opened the floodgates of German conquest when, for the sake of overruling Bonnet, he advised Chamberlain to travel to Berchtesgaden and, in that manner, assumed responsibility for the first meeting of the British Prime Minister with the Führer on September 15. Afterward how could we expect to dam the torrent? But the ensuing moral catastrophe redounded to the guilt of Bonnet—of Bonnet, who had re-entered the negotiation with a vengeance. Upon the conclusion of the Munich Agreement the Franco-British guarantee of Czechoslovakia's new frontiers had automatically become effective. Immediately, as we have seen, Bonnet cast to the winds France's signed obligation. Thus we were stripped for the future of all diplomatic defense. Who could ever again trust our pledged word?

The Russians quickly drew their own conclusions: the Third Republic's promises of help no longer had any value for anyone. The Franco-Soviet Treaty of May 2, 1935, had no more substance than a scrap of paper. Neither on September 15, when Chamberlain left for Berchtesgaden, nor on the twenty-second, when he went to Godesberg, nor on the twenty-eighth, when the British and French proposed their conference, had the Russians been notified in time—they who were allies or at least associates.

The abiding, the mystic faith in "Munich" so widely instilled by Bonnet, the belief in a sure prospect of peace attested before the public by his journalists, was a fraud. It was a fraud because the public was never told that some precarious peace could be had only if France, once for all, turned her back on eastern Europe—and this was a deadly policy.

All the camouflage used at the time won't blind us to the fact that Bonnet and also Chamberlain had settled on that policy. . . .

To appraise the damage done we need only consider our respective positions on September 15 and on December 6, at the starting point and at the culmination of the so-called Munich policy. In December, France no longer had a single sure ally at her side. Czechoslovakia was moribund; Colonel Beck's pro-Germanism still held Poland in its grip; Russia, it is true, had not explicitly given up the 1935 treaty with France, but, according to one of her leaders, this was solely in the vague hope that the now empty shell might somehow scare off the Germans. In London a member of Parliament exclaimed, "It is not wise to go tiger hunting with the French!" . . .

[The third accusation, that "Bonnet, having cast our alliances overboard, drifted toward war without winning them back," is concerned with the period after Munich.]

II. HISTORICAL JUDGMENTS

Martin Gilbert

MUNICH AND THE NEW APPEASEMENT

Munich has generally been regarded as the high point of appeasement, but Martin Gilbert attempts to show that the appeasement of Munich was quite different from the older forms, although linked with them in Great Britain by some common characteristics. The author was a Research Scholar at St. Antony's College, Oxford, and has been a Fellow of Merton College, Oxford, since 1962. In 1965 he was a visiting Professor at South Carolina for five months. He was appointed Official Biographer of Sir Winston Churchill in 1968. Prior to the publication of his work on appeasement, he published with Richard Gott *The Appeasers*, a study of British foreign policy before and after Munich. He has also written *The European Powers, 1900–1945,* and *Britain and Germany Between the Wars,* among other works. Does his exposition of appeasement help to clarify the issues in the Munich debate?

APPEASEMENT and "Munich" were quite different phenomena. Appeasement was a traditional policy, based upon concessions made from a position of strength. "Munich" was much more an emergency plan, intended to buy peace at the expense of the disintegration of Czechoslovakia and the transfer, without plebiscite, of non-Nazis to Nazi rule. Appeasement's justification, whether at the time of the American Revolution or of the Lausanne Conference on reparations, was that it was rooted in a deep concern for considerations of international morality, and that however expedient specific acts of appeasement might be, they were also moral. "Munich" may have been expedient; but it had less of an aura of morality. Hitler's rejection of the Runciman Mission removed the Czech crisis from the traditional sphere of legitimate Treaty revision to a new world of threats, tension, and emergency.

Certain aspects of the new appeasement had also been present in the old. Fear of communism certainly spanned the two, and the nervousness provoked by the murder of the Tsar, the Red Army's attack on Warsaw and the "Zinoviev letter" was accentuated by the much publicized Stalinist purges from 1936–8, by the Russian involvement in the Spanish Civil War, albeit in defence of the legitimate republican government, and by the belief that Russia would use a Czechoslovak-German war in order to advance Russian interests in central Europe through her alliance with Prague. Chamberlain may not have been as tempestuously anti-communist in 1937 as Churchill had been in 1919, but he was sufficiently distrustful of Soviet intentions to doubt even Churchill's insistence, as well as that of Lloyd George, that an Anglo-Russian alliance was perhaps the only way of deterring German aggression in 1939.

Suspicion of France was also a link between appeasement old and new. Before 1935 French anti-Germanism was resented as being the supposed cause of European tensions. After 1935, as German rearmament increased, France became an object of derision: surely no reliance could be placed, it was argued, upon a tired nation, weary of war, unwilling to pit her army and resources

From Martin Gilbert, *The Roots of Appeasement* (London, 1966), pp. 179–187. Reprinted by permission of the author.

against the greater power of Germany. French defeatism, much evident after 1935, made alliance and even co-operation with France seem a risky venture, just as, before 1935, French alliances in eastern Europe had queered the value of her friendship. Nor did Léon Blum's Popular Front government improve the French image in British eyes after 1936. It seemed an incitement to overt class antagonism and an invitation to civil war. The cry of the French right, "better Hitler than Blum," warned British politicians of the dangers of relying in a crisis upon French solidarity or consistency. Churchill insisted, in his public speeches, upon the need to maintain close Anglo-French co-operation. But more than twenty years of anti-French feeling in Britain augmented the arguments of those who at the time of Munich said that France could not be relied upon to act with Britain in any anti-German or pro-Czech policy. The new appeasement lacked the full flavour of international amity and mutual confidence, which, particularly under MacDonald, permeated the old.

A third consistent theme in inter-war foreign policy was the need of successive Governments to work in harmony with the British Empire. The fall of Lloyd George, following Canadian, Australian, and South African hostility to his Chanak policy, seemed to point a warning finger at the dangers of getting out of step with imperial sentiment. Probably these fears were exaggerated: certainly the Locarno agreements, which in theory could have involved Britain in a European war to defend either France or Germany from attack, were negotiated without imperial participation or prior approval, and yet the Empire survived. To strengthen imperial links, Ramsay MacDonald and Baldwin had accepted Imperial Preference in 1932, at the expense, as both Vansittart and Ashton-Gwatkin, pointed out at the time, of intervening beneficially, and perhaps decisively, to halt European economic disintegration. Neville Chamberlain seemed to take the wishes of the Empire as seriously as his two immediate predecessors. At the Imperial Conference of 1937 he was struck by the majority view among the Dominion Prime Ministers that a firm imperial commitment to resist Hitler by force could not be given. . . .

During the Munich crisis the Dominion Prime Ministers made it clear that they did not regard a German attack on Czechoslovakia as an adequate reason for the Empire becoming involved in a European war. No doubt this view, which was expressed forcibly and repeatedly, influenced Chamberlain, and helped to determine British policy. The imperial armies had played a crucial part in the Great War, and had suffered heavy casualties. Passchendaele and Gallipoli were a long way from Toronto, Sydney, and Cape Town. If Chamberlain himself, from London, could describe Czechoslovakia as "a far-away country," it is not surprising that Dominion politicians could not conceive of it as an acceptable *casus belli.*

Attitudes to Russia, France, and the Empire linked the old appeasement with the new. But the new appeasement was influenced also by factors and emotions absent before 1937, which counteracted the growing belief in German immorality. The new factor was Germany's growing military and air power. The new emotion was fear. Simultaneously, weakness and fear propelled the Government forward, both to the policy of making concessions, and to rearmament. Pro-Germanism, dislike of Versailles, trust in Nazi goodwill, hope in Hitler's reformation; these influences for appeasement all survived. But over them hung the grey cloud of fear, which covered all acts of appeasement after 1937 with a shadow of doubt, hesitation, and uncertainty. All who supported appeasement, but knew Britain's military weakness, and Chamberlain was one of them, could no longer embark upon a policy beneficial to Germany, even in the short term, without serious anxiety. The firmness of moral purpose that had invigorated appeasement from 1918 to at least 1935, had disappeared almost entirely by the time of the *Anschluss* in 1938. . . . The leading politicians and other advocates of the new appeasement were of lesser ability than the majority of their predecessors after 1918. Neville Chamberlain was certainly a man of great determination, but he was also obstinate to the point of blindness, and unimaginative. Lord Halifax, his Foreign Secretary after February 1938, was a man of uncertain judgement and vacillating opinions. Henderson, his principal source of information about German moods and intentions, was erratic, vain, muddle-headed, and at times almost hysterical. All three believed in the possibility of saving Anglo-German relations from the storm, caused by rearmament, *Anschluss*, and anti-semitism, into which international relations had been swept. But these three men did not have the ability or the knowledge to act as successful navigators. Of the Prime Minister himself, Lord Strang, who had accompanied him to Munich, wrote in retrospect:

It can fairly be said of Neville Chamberlain that he was not well versed in foreign affairs, that he had no touch for a diplomatic situation, that he did not fully realize what it was he was doing, and that his naive confidence in his own judgement and powers of persuasion and achievement was misplaced.

This was not the judgement of a hostile or carping critic, but of a man whose sympathies were entirely with the belief in the need for compromise and conciliation in international affairs. The same is true of Lord Birkenhead, Halifax's admirer and biographer, and in 1938 his Parliamentary Private Secretary who, when confronted in 1965 with the evidence of his friend's Foreign Secretaryship wrote of how

His instinct in an explosive situation was to conciliate. When nations or men became inflamed with passion, he did not catch fire . . . a certain sluggishness of imagination prevented him ever receiving a blinding realization of terrible events. . . . Edward was thus not fitted by nature to preside over the Foreign Office at such a moment of history.

Halifax was not blind. He knew, not only from the newspapers, that Hitler was capable of great brutality. Many of the British protests against concentration camp excesses were sent to Germany through the Foreign Office. Halifax had read of the cruelties perpetrated by the Nazis after the annexation of Austria; he had received full reports on the crude anti-semitic policies by which Jews became "second-class" citizens and were made to suffer numerous indignities and hardships. At the time of the Munich Agreement he expressed in Cabinet his distaste of a policy which involved forcing a democratic state to make concessions to a totalitarian one. But the troubles of Halifax's conscience were not sufficient to persuade Chamberlain to alter, or even to modify, his policy. As Lord Birkenhead wrote, Halifax, "failed to induce in the Prime Minister the sense of urgency demanded by the hour, or to exert on him a more powerful influence which he alone in the Cabinet could have commanded."

The only other source from which a warning might have come was Nevile Henderson, the British Ambassador in Berlin. But Henderson was a man driven by anxiety and prejudice into a pro-German position. He considered the Czechs "a pig-headed race," on whose behalf Britain should make no efforts whatsoever. Regarding the very existence of Czechoslovakia as a mistake, he wanted Treaty revision in Germany's favour to be the cornerstone of British policy. He felt that it was immoral for Britain to do anything that might keep German-speaking people outside the frontiers of Nazi Germany. He did not pause to ask whether Sudeten Jews, communists, socialists, liberals, or devout Christians would want union with a Germany whose philosophy and actions cast them in the role of unwanted, degenerate "scum," or would at once restrict, as in the case of authors, actors, musicians or journalists, the things they could publish or perform. According to Henderson:

There can never be appeasement in Europe so long as Czechoslovakia remains the link with Moscow and hostile to Germany. Czechoslovakia can never enjoy a moment's peace so long as she remains the enemy of Germany It is a case of the inexorable logic of geographic position. If she wants to survive at all she must come economically within the orbit of Germany. We poor mortals can kick against logic but we can never prevail against it in the end.

The appeasement whose "logic" Henderson upheld was not that which had appealed to his predecessor, Lord D'Abernon; nor were Henderson's reports on the German internal situation as perceptive as those of his two other forerunners in Berlin, Rumbold and Phipps. Orme Sargent, who saw Henderson's dispatches as they reached the Foreign Office, and whose "Sargent chain" had been a blueprint for appeasement before the advent of Hitler, was horrified by what he read. In retrospect he wrote of Henderson that he

. . . had no preconceived dislike of authoritarian government as such, and was therefore ready to believe that Great Britain and Germany could be reconciled even if this meant tacit acquiescence by Britain in the adoption by Germany of the Nazi philosophy of life and system of government as well as the aggrandizement of Germany in Central Europe.

This was the gravamen of the contemporary charge against Chamberlain's appeasement; not that conciliation was wrong, or that Treaty revision was wrong, as general guidelines for a liberal and Christian policy, but that such a base was unrealistic when applied to Nazi Germany in 1938. Hitler had been given the benefit of every doubt for five years. He had been offered concessions, including colonial and economic concessions greatly to his advantage, but had preferred the path of unilateral action, surprise, the threat of violence, vituperative language and overt brutality. The old appeasement was rooted in a belief that Britain and Germany had much in common; that their interests often coincided and that their civilizations were in no way incompatible. Neither premise fitted the situation in 1938. . . .

Munich was not appeasement's finest hour, but its most perverted. It was a distortion of all that appeasement stood for. It was a conference without compromise; public speeches without moderation; a final judgment without the principal party, Czechoslovakia, being allowed

to be present; a solution which hurt as many people as it benefited and whetted the appetites it had been intended to satisfy; populations transferred without a plebiscite; a sacrifice in interests without a *quid pro quo;* a pandering to immorality without convincing evidence of imminent better times. . . . Among the most telling criticisms were those of Harold Nicolson, whose book *Peacemaking 1919* had done so much, in the very year that Hitler came to power, to confirm public opinion in its belief that Germany had been ill-served at the Paris Peace Conference. Speaking in the House of Commons after Munich, Nicolson criticized those who considered the new appeasement a sign of realism, and who saw compromise with Nazi Germany as a viable, and desirable policy:

I know that in these days of realism principles are considered as rather eccentric and ideals are identified with hysteria. I know that those of us who believe in the traditions of our policy, who believe in the precepts which we have inherited from our ancestors, who believe that one great function of this country is to maintain moral standards in Europe, to maintain a settled pattern of international relations, not to make friends with people who are demonstrably evil, not to go out of our way to make friends with them but to set up some sort of standard by which the smaller powers can test what is good in international conduct and what is not—I know that those who hold such beliefs are accused of possessing the Foreign Office mind. I thank God that I possess the Foreign Office mind.

"Munich" and appeasement have both become words of disapproval and abuse. For nearly thirty years they have been linked together as the twin symbols of British folly. Together they have been defended as if they were inseparable. Yet "Munich" was a policy, dictated by fear and weakness, which Neville Chamberlain devised as a means, not of postponing war but, as he personally believed, of making Anglo-German war unnecessary in the future. Appeasement was quite different; it was a policy of constant concessions based on common sense and strength. Whereas the debate over the wisdom of Chamberlain's actions will continue, and the believers in his vision cross swords for many years to come with those who consider his actions short-sighted, unrealistic, and dangerous, the debate over appeasement deserves a different fate.

Although appeasement failed when confronted with the aggressive, irresponsible behaviour of Nazi Germany, it did not, because of this failure become retrospectively mistaken. It was never a mis-guided policy, even if it became, by 1938, temporarily an unrealistic one. International affairs do from time to time reach an *impasse* on account of the total impossibility of agreement between two conflicting States. But the norm of international affairs remains the assumption that agreement is possible. For as long as this assumption holds good, appeasement is a necessary policy, combining expediency with morality.

Iain Macleod

NEVILLE CHAMBERLAIN DEFENDED

Although Georges Bonnet lived to write his own defense, Neville Chamberlain has left only his speeches and private papers from which to interpret his policy. Iain Macleod, a member of the House of Commons since 1950 and active for more than twenty years in the Conservative Party organization, has utilized these papers and other sources in his study of the former Conservative leader. In his discussion of Chamberlain's policy in the Munich crisis Macleod has sought to counter the major criticisms launched at the time and since by its opponents and students. The result is a sober exposition which admits neither blundering nor tragic necessity, but assesses the Munich Agreement as a wise action which bought time for the Western powers. Is his reasoning convincing, or has he fallen into the temptation of biographers to make his subject a hero without blame?

I F Austria goes," Austen Chamberlain had warned in 1936, "Czechoslovakia is indefensible." Two years later this was the considered and consistent verdict of the Committee of Imperial Defence and the Chiefs of Staff, and of the Foreign Office experts to whom the question was submitted.

N.C. to Ida 20.3.1938 [Chamberlain to his sister Ida]
You have only to look at the map to see that nothing that France or we could do could possibly save Czechoslovakia from being overrun by the Germans if they wanted to do it. The Austrian frontier is practically open; the great Skoda munition works are within easy bombing distance of the German aerodromes, the railways all pass through German territory, Russia is 100 miles away. Therefore we could not help Czechoslovakia—she would simply be a pretext for going to war with Germany. That we could not think of unless we had a reasonable prospect of being able to beat her to her knees in a reasonable time, and of that I see no sign. I have therefore abandoned any idea of giving guarantees to Czechoslovakia, or to France in connection with her obligations to that country.

[Why did Chamberlain not seek Russian cooperation?]
. . . What assistance Russia was in fact prepared to give was always in doubt. As late as September 23rd, our Foreign Under-Secretary, R. A. Butler, who was at Geneva, could get nothing more precise out of Litvinov than that if the French came to the assistance of the Czechs the Russians "would take action" and "might desire to raise the matter in the League." Time and again, the appreciations arriving at the Foreign Office from our Embassy in Moscow warned that the great purges of 1937 had had a "disastrous effect on the morale and also on the efficiency of the Red Army" and that "it is unlikely that the Soviet Union will go to war in defence of Czechoslovakia." Precisely similar appreciations were reaching Berlin from the German Ambassador, who reported that the overwhelming conviction of the diplomatic corps in Moscow was that the Soviet would do as little as possible. A post-war historian of Soviet foreign policy confirms that there is very little evidence that in the summer of 1938 the Russians were preparing

From Iain Macleod, *Neville Chamberlain* (London: Frederick Muller, 1961), pp. 224, 226–229, 240–241, 257–262, 267–272. Reprinted by permission of the author.

their own people for the possibility that they would be involved in war. Chamberlain's own view was that Stalin was "stealthily and cunningly pulling all the strings behind the scenes to get us involved in war with Germany," a war in which he hoped to be the *tertius gaudens*. Soviet policy when Germany attacked Poland the next year scarcely contradicted this diagnosis.

A second and more substantial criticism of Chamberlain's diplomacy was made by Daladier, the new French Prime Minister, who came to London at the end of April to urge "that war could only be avoided if Great Britain and France made their determination quite clear to maintain the peace of Europe by respecting the liberties and the rights of independent peoples."

There were great attractions in such a declaration if it could be implemented, but whether Daladier spoke for his Cabinet, let alone for France, was more than doubtful. Strang, then head of the Central Department of the Foreign Office, recalls that "unlike the British Government, the French Government were deeply divided, with Georges Mandel and his friends all for resistance and Georges Bonnet and his like all for surrender, and with Edouard Daladier . . . torn between the two, leaning towards a robust policy but lacking the resolution to hold to it. The result was that, while the declared policy of France was to stand by her obligation, a very different impression was given by what French Ministers said behind the scenes, whether in social gatherings or to foreign representatives." They were inevitably conscious of the military and moral weaknesses of the nation at their back. The brunt of the war would fall first upon the French. Yet La Chambre, who was Air Minister at the time, stated without contradiction at the Riom Trials that it was impossible for the French air forces in 1938 to carry out effectively even the very limited duties laid down by the General Staff. The French had a clear treaty obligation to the Czechs; for them a point of honour, not simply a point of strategy, was involved. Yet *Gringoire's* celebrated head-

line, "*Veux-tu mourir pour le Tchecoslovaquie?*" was typical of the pacifism of their press from the start. On April 8th the German Ambassador in Paris, Welczeck, reported that the declarations of the French Government found little echo in press or public opinion. By the eve of the Munich Conference our own Ambassador in Paris, Sir Eric Phipps, was reporting: "All that is best in France is against war, *almost* at any price (hence the really deep and pathetic gratitude shown to our Prime Minister)." Phipps added: "To embark upon what will presumably be the biggest conflict in history with our ally, who will fight, if fight she must, without eyes (air force) and without real heart must surely give us furiously to think. It may be asked why I have not reported sooner in the above sense. The answer is that up to the last hour the French had hypnotised themselves into believing that peace depended upon Great Britain, and not upon Herr Hitler. They were convinced, that is to say, that if Great Britain spoke with sufficient firmness Herr Hitler would collapse." Chamberlain was never prepared to act on this assumption. Later that summer he was fortified in his attitude by reading Professor Harold Temperley's book on the foreign policy of Canning, who had laid it down repeatedly, "that you should never menace unless you are in a position to carry out your threats." This in effect was what Chamberlain had said to Daladier on April 29th.

"If he had understood M. Daladier correctly," says the official record, "the latter was of the opinion that, if, at this juncture, we were to speak to the German Government with sufficient firmness, then there would be no war, for either Germany would not be able or would not care to brave the united forces of France, Great Britain and Czechoslovakia, and such assistance as might be obtainable from outside sources. He consided that this was what the Americans in their card games called bluff. It amounted to advancing a certain declaration in the hope that that declaration would prevent the events we did not wish to occur. But it was not a certainty that such action would be successful. It might be true that the chances against war were 100–1, but so long as that one chance existed we must consider carefully what our attitude must be, and how we should be prepared to act in the event of war. . . . If a war arose after such a declaration, he himself could not see any possibility of saving Czechoslovakia, of avoiding the destruction of that country, or of its being overrun by the aggressor. . . . In such a situation, were we to say to Germany that we would not tolerate her continued progress in Europe and that the moment had come to call a halt; and that, if Germany were to take certain steps, we would then declare war? We would then be casting the die and deciding that, in our view, this was, from the military point of view, the opportune moment to declare war on Germany with the object of bringing about her defeat. When listening to M. Daladier, he had himself felt corresponding emotions. It made his blood boil to see Germany getting away with it time after time and increasing her domination over free peoples. But such sentimental considerations were dangerous, and he must remember, as M. Daladier would also have to remember, the forces with which we were playing. Whatever the odds might be in favour of peace or war, it was not money but men with which we were gambling, and he could not lightly enter into a conflict which might mean such frightful results for innumerable families, men, women and children, of our own race. We must therefore consider with the greatest care whether, if the attitude he had just outlined towards Germany were adopted, we—and in this connexion he was thinking of His Majesty's Government and the French Government, since we could not count on any outside support—were sufficiently powerful to make victory certain. Frankly, he did not think we were."

To this piece of rigorous reasoning he added, if only implicitly, a consideration of almost equal importance. It was true, he said to the French, that at some time we might be compelled to go to war. "Circumstances might arise in which things more precious would be at stake than wealth, or life, or property." The Czechoslovak crisis, to his mind, did not fulfil these conditions of last resort.

The problem, as Mussolini pithily put it in a speech at Treviso in September, was that Czechoslovakia was not just Czechoslovakia, but "Czecho-Germano-Polono-Magyaro-Rutheno-Roumano-Slovakia." Its boundaries had been drawn by the Treaty of Versailles in defiance of the doctrine of self-determination, and it reproduced in miniature the whole racial jigsaw of the old Habsburg Empire. Lloyd George had had "serious misgivings" about this, but the persuasive Benes had won the day by promising the Peace Conference to organise the minorities on a cantonal system analogous to that of Switzerland. This promise was not fulfilled.

* * *

The documents we have accumulated since the war make plain the unwavering persistence with which Chamberlain pushed through this policy [Sudeten right of self-determination, an international commission to fix the new frontiers, and their guarantee internationally in place of Czech alliances with France and Russia]. His mind, once made up, was always extremely hard to alter, and on this issue it was made up early. Either there had to be concessions, or else we had to go to war. But how *could* we go to war, when we ourselves were unready, when the French were blowing hot and cold, when the Russians could not be relied upon, and when the Dominions— South Africa, Australia and Canada— were divided? And why *need* we go to war, on account of "a quarrel in a faraway country between people of whom we know nothing," in the absence of any direct treaty obligation on our part, and in order to compel three million Germans to remain Czechoslovak subjects against their interest and will?

But, ask the critics, was the choice really as simple and clear-cut as Chamberlain thought? Was there not behind the brazen front which Germany presented to the world an element of bluff or internal stress which a firmer British policy could have exploited? Would an ultimatum for Czechoslovakia have stopped Hitler in his tracks or led to his overthrow by his own military leaders? Chamberlain certainly had an inkling of dissension in the German camp. He knew, from the Foreign Office telegrams, that General Beck had resigned after a stormy interview with Hitler, because he declined to participate in an attack on a friendly State. He had also read the account of Vansittart's private conversation with a Herr von Kleist who came to England in August with, it was said, the approval of the German War Office, as "a representative of the old German Conservative Party" and "an emissary of the moderates in the General Staff." "He reminds me," wrote Chamberlain to Halifax, "of the Jacobites at the court of France in King William's time and I think we must discount a good deal of what he says." Would, or should, his attitude have been different had he actually got wind of General Halder's now celebrated plot to arrest Hitler in the event of Czechoslovakia being invaded? "All conspiracies are difficult," replied Sir Lewis Namier, scarcely a friendly witness so far as Chamberlain is concerned, "and this one must be counted among the unhatched chickens. Moreover, the German generals seem to have been singularly inept at conspiracy; never before had they practised that manoeuvre, and now it was too late to learn it." This view is closely confirmed in Sir John Wheeler-Bennett's brilliant history of the German Army, which records the conclusion that "there is no evidence but the flimsiest assertion that, had Mr. Chamberlain never gone to Berchtesgaden or to Godesberg or to Munich, the conspirators would have been sufficiently prepared or resolute to strike. As for Hitler himself, there is no ground at all for supposing that he was bluffing or, therefore, that Chamberlain could successfully have "called his bluff." "On the contrary," concludes Sir Ivone Kirkpatrick, who was then First Secretary in the Berlin Embassy, "he was not only resolved on war but was actually looking forward to it." The proof of this was given at Godesberg.

* * *

The arguments about Munich will continue, but it is possible now that the archives have been opened and so many private accounts published to judge them in perspective. Few people seriously claim now that a League of Nations with more than half the great powers outside it would have or could have stopped the Second World War. No-one seriously claims who has studied their speeches, particularly in the General Election of 1935, that the Labour Party would have pushed rearmament ahead faster, or indeed anything like so fast, as Chamberlain did in 1936 and 1937. In their television appearance together in the autumn of 1959, on the occasion of Mr. Eisenhower's visit to London, both Mr. Macmillan and Mr. Eisenhower agreed that the Second World War was inevitable because Hitler was determined on it, and the evidence that this was in fact so is now overwhelming. Should then Britain have fought in October 1938 rather than September 1939? Was the year's respite a gain on balance to Great Britain or the Axis Powers? And here one of the most interesting witnesses is Mr. John F. Kennedy, the President of the United States. His father was at the time the American Ambassador at the Court of St. James, and felt deep despondency in 1940 about Britain's chances of survival. His son did not share this view and (aged 23) put forward his own. This is his judgement [*Why England Slept* (1940), pp. 195–196]:

[People] felt and many still do feel that Hitler in 1938 was merely bluffing. . . . Many in England shared this belief even in August 1939. There, people felt Chamberlain was badly taken in, but I think a study of the position of the two countries will show that Chamberlain could not have fought even if he had wanted to. I do not claim that Munich was simply the result of British inability to fight as set forth by Baron von Neurath. I believe that Chamberlain was sincere in thinking that a great step had been taken towards healing one of Europe's fever sores. I believe that English public opinion was not sufficiently aroused to back him in a war. Most people in England felt "It's not worth a war to prevent the Sudeten Germans from going back to Germany." They failed at that time to see the larger issue, involving the domination of Europe. But though all these factors played a part in the settlement of Munich, I feel that Munich was inevitable on the grounds of lack of armaments alone.

It is not at Munich but at the locust years, 1934 and 1935, that the finger of criticism should be pointed. Too little was done, even though Chamberlain was the most valiant for rearmament in the Government—so much so that the contrast of his tough attitude with Baldwin's more pliant one brought stern condemnation from *The Economist* in October 1935:

It is certainly a regrettable departure from British tradition that the Chancellor of the Exchequer should himself be the foremost advocate of increased expenditure on armaments. And it certainly will not help to promote national agreement on foreign policy if collective security is to be used as an excuse for unilateral rearmament by Great Britain.

It is fair to add, as Mr. Kennedy does, that *The Economist* later changed its mind, but also, again following Mr. Kennedy, that rearmament policies cannot change as swiftly as editorial views.

We can now check Mr. Kennedy's assessment against the known facts and figures of military production at the time.

Eleven months separated the Munich Agreement from the outbreak of war. Diplomatically, the period falls into two equal and distinct parts, divided by the death blow which Hitler delivered to Czechoslovakia and to the policy of appeasement in March 1939. "A new epoch in the course of our foreign policy," to use Chamberlain's own description, opened after the occupation of Prague. The military turning point, however, antedated the diplomatic. "A new epoch

in the history of rearmament," to quote the echoing phrase of the historian of British war production, "began in the autumn of 1938 and ended in the summer of 1940." After Munich, that is to say, rearmament was "definitely geared to eventual military action," and the last strong hopes of peace were not allowed to hold back our accelerating preparations against war.

"One good thing, at any rate, has come out of this emergency through which we have passed," said Chamberlain at the end of the Munich debate in the House of Commons. "It has thrown a vivid light upon our preparations for defence, on their strength and on their weakness. I should not think we were doing our duty if we had not already ordered that a prompt and thorough inquiry should be made to cover the whole of our preparations, military and civil, in order to see, in the light of what has happened during these hectic days, what further steps may be necessary to make good our deficiencies in the shortest possible time."

The deficiency upon which public and Parliamentary attention chiefly and rightly focused was in our defence against air attack, including civil defence. . . .

The year's breathing-space was also vital for the modernization and expansion of our air power. . . . In September 1938, the R.A.F. had only one operational fighter squadron equipped with Spitfires and five in process of being equipped with Hurricanes; by the summer of 1939, however, it had 26 squadrons of modern eight-gun fighters, and a year later during the Battle of Britain it was to have on average 47. . . .

Though the numerical increase in the total strength of the Luftwaffe during this period was at least as great as that of the R.A.F., the extent to which we caught up with the Germans in modernising the quality of our fighter force has been authoritatively described as "the most important achievement of rearmament between Munich and the outbreak of war." This great gain was freely admitted by Churchill in *The Gathering Storm*. But Churchill went on to make a powerful argument that 1938 nevertheless presented us with a more favourable military situation than 1939, since the Germans would have found it less easy then to win bases in France and the Low Countries from which to raid Britain with decisive effect. I doubt, however, if he gives sufficient weight to contemporary estimates of the vulnerability of London and other nerve centres in 1938. More important, the argument rests upon assumptions of Allied, or rather French, military superiority at that date which are, to say the least, controversial. The contrary considerations are economically deployed in an entry in Hore-Belisha's diary a few days before the Munich settlement:

The P.M. yesterday spoke to us of the horrors of war, of German bombers over London and of his horror in allowing our people to suffer all the miseries of war in our present state. No-one is more conscious than I am of our present deficiencies. Chiefs of Staff view—to take offensive against Germany now would be like "a man attacking a tiger before he has loaded his gun."

* * *

Military considerations, however, can only be part of the argument. Whatever view one may take of the military consequences of the "Munich year," of its effect on the will to fight of the country and the Empire there can be no doubt. In 1936, the year of the Rhineland crisis, when we might have stopped Hitler in his tracks, the representative British view was that the Germans were "only going into their own back garden." In 1938, a denial of self-determination to three million Germans living under alien rule was not considered either here or in the Empire to be something "that Britons should be asked to die for." In 1939, on the other hand, it had become plain beyond doubt that the ambitions of Nazism stretched far beyond the ethnic frontiers of Germany, that it had indeed "made up its mind to dominate the world by fear of its force." Here, far more than in the precise stages to which German rearmament or our rearmament had advanced, we may

discern what determined the date of our declaration of war. At the heart of Chamberlain's policy lay the fundamental proposition he expressed at the end of the Munich debate in a moving passage on the dread features of modern warfare. "You cannot ask people to accept a prospect of that kind, you cannot force them into a position that they have got to accept it," he declared, "unless you feel yourself, and can make them feel, that the cause for which they are going to fight is a vital cause—a cause that transcends all the human values, a cause to which you can point, if some day you win the victory, and say, 'That cause is safe'." This was certainly what the nation did feel in the autumn of 1939 and did not feel at the time of Munich. As Lord Halifax put it:

. . . when all has been said, one fact remains dominant and unchallengeable. When war did come a year later it found a country and Commonwealth wholly united within itself, convinced to the foundations of soul and conscience that every conceivable effort has been made to find the way of sparing Europe the ordeal of war, and that no alternative remained. And that was the big thing that Chamberlain did.

No-one can dispute that the avoidance of war in 1938 was in accord with the overwhelming sentiment of British opinion. . . . The British Press was certainly reflecting the mood of the nation. Argument grew hotter as time went on but it has been very properly pointed out that in the Commons debate after Munich the Opposition virtually evaded the issue of peace and war:

Just as, on September 28th, no one of them had interrupted Mr. Chamberlain's speech to protest against the acceptance of the Berchtesgaden terms, so now, with one exception—Mr. Duff Cooper—no Member of the House was sufficiently certain of himself to stand up in his place and say that the terms of the Munich Agreement should have been rejected at the price of war, because no Member of the House was sufficiently assured that the people of Britain would have endorsed such a rejection.

Nor would the people of the Dominions have endorsed such a rejection.

No-one who sat in this place, as I did during the autumn of '38, with almost daily visitations from eminent Canadians and Australians, could fail to realise that war with Germany at that time would have been misunderstood and resented from end to end of the Empire

—this was written by Geoffrey Dawson, editor of *The Times*, in a letter to Chamberlain which arrived the day after he died. Mackenzie King of Canada told Churchill during the war "that he very much doubted whether his country would have rallied to us at once." Though the Australian Government considered that constitutionally it was not possible for Australia to be neutral in a British war, the Opposition were flatly against involvement in 1938. So far as South Africa was concerned, Hertzog and Smuts were agreed on a policy of non-belligerency. . . .

Not only from all over Britain and the Dominions but from all over the world the tributes poured into Downing Street. Within three weeks of Munich he had received more than 40,000 letters and his wife another 12,000 and not until after Christmas did this tide show much abatement. Accompanying the messages came flowers, and some poems, and gifts galore—with a strong emphasis, as might be expected, on fishing rods and salmon flies. Four thousand tulips arrived from Holland, cases of Alsatian wines from France, and from Greece a request for a piece of his umbrella to make a relic in an icon. King Haakon of Norway cabled his congratulations and King Leopold of the Belgians wrote in his own hand. From countless Englishmen in public life we may take two quotations. "You have done a most wonderful piece of work and done it under the guidance and providence of God," declared George Lansbury who once had led the Labour Party; and the Archbishop of Canterbury: "You have been enabled to do a great thing in a great way at a time of almost unexampled crisis. I thank God for it." More impressive still were the

letters from humbler folk, from total strangers, from private soldiers of the First World War, from those who had been unemployed for years yet still managed to send him a present in gratitude. Most touching of all were the thoughts of the women with most to lose. From Hampshire: "I feel with God's help that you have given me back my boys, at one time it seemed as if we must lose all three of them"; from Northumberland: "I thank you a thousand times from the depth of my heart, the mother of five sons": from Paris: "Il n'y a pas une épouse, pas une maman de France qui, à l'heure présente, ne vous vénère et prie pour vous et ceux que vous aimez"*; and from Rome: "Mister Chamberlain! God may bless your white head! I am an Italian mother who wishes express you all her devotion."

This is what that great-hearted Socialist James Maxton meant when he said during the Munich debate that the Prime Minister had done "something that the mass of the common people in the world wanted done." From his very different standpoint, Anthony Eden meant the same thing when he counted among the influences that had averted war, "that genuine desire for peace among all peoples, German and Italian, as well as French and British." Wherever Chamberlain went in the months that followed the truth of these observations was underlined. In the towns and villages of South Wales—scarcely a conservative stronghold—"I never heard a solitary boo"; on the contrary "the streets were lined with people cheering and shouting 'Good old Neville' and 'God bless you' with the most evident sincerity and heartiness." In Paris, in November, and still more in Rome, in January, the warmth of his reception was particularly remarkable.

Eden, during the Munich debate, had acknowledged the significance of the spontaneous ovations which Chamberlain had been accorded in Germany. "It was clearly a manifestation of the deep

* "There is not a wife nor a mother in France who, at the present time, does not venerate you and pray for you and for those whom you love." [Editor's note.]

desire of the German people for peace," he said; and added, "the fact that it has at last found expression may be a real signpost on the road to peace." This was Chamberlain's thought too; and, if he erred, it was in holding to this thought too obsessively, too obstinately, hoping against hope, even when every other signpost began to point the other way. It is not true that he trusted too much in Hitler; what he trusted in too much were the many deterrent and persuasive forces that might have been expected to hold Hitler back. . . .

Even when the assurances given at Munich had been thrown to the winds by Hitler, and Prague occupied, Chamberlain still refused to accept the view that war was inevitable. He trusted rather in the deterrent effect of the guarantees now made to Poland, Roumania, Greece and Turkey. He trusted, as ever, in the restraints of more moderate opinion inside Germany.

D. C. Watt

THE COMMONWEALTH AND MUNICH

Member of the Department of International History at the London School of Economics and Political Science and editor of the 1965 *Survey of International Affairs,* D. C. Watt is a careful and percipient student of contemporary British and European history. His essay on "The Influence of the Commonwealth on British Foreign Policy," from which this selection is taken, does not attempt to praise or blame the British statesmen who were responsible for the Munich policy, but to add another explanation of why they acted as they did. Does the attitude of the Commonwealth mean that Munich was a "tragic necessity," at least for the British government?

FROM the moment the Anschluss with Austria was successfully achieved, it was clear that a crisis over Czechoslovakia was imminent. The British attitude throughout this crisis remained absolutely unchanged. To the French and the Czechs, emphasis was laid on Britain's determination not to become involved in central European problems by guaranteeing Czechoslovakia's frontiers. In the British view, the conflict lay essentially between the Czech Government and her minorities, the danger being that Hitler's notoriously violent passions might lead him to seize an occasion to intervene and annex the Sudetenland as he had Austria. If he did act in this fashion, neither the Czechs nor their French and Soviet allies could rely on automatic support from Britain. The British were not prepared to fight a war to keep the Sudeten Germans under Czech rule. To the Germans on the other hand, the British emphasized that should Hitler choose the way of the sword rather than negotiation, he could not rely on Britain standing aloof. If he risked war, then he must risk it spreading beyond those immediately involved.

* * *

During the September days the Dominions governments were kept fully informed of the situation both by direct telegrams to the Dominions capitals and by almost daily meetings between the High Commissioners and Malcolm MacDonald, the Secretary of State for the Dominions. The main lead in representations to the British Government was taken by the Australian and South African High Commissioners, Bruce and Te Water. The Canadian High Commissioner, Vincent Massey, spoke without instructions from his government, who under the leadership of Mackenzie King deliberately refused to take any line whatever, but there can be little doubt that he spoke for much of Canadian opinion. The Irish High Commissioner, Dulanty, took the same line as his Australian and South African colleagues. The New Zealand High Commissioner chose to spend the whole month of the crisis in Geneva, which can hardly have been without his government's approval. The High Commissioners thoroughly approved Chamberlain's policy, exerting pressure only when it looked as if the British Government were abandoning its hopes of a settlement and resigning itself to conflict. Two out of the four, Vincent Massey and Bruce, were in close contact with Dawson and *The Times.*

The main weight of their representa-

From D. C. Watt, *Personalities and Politics* (Notre Dame, Indiana: The University of Notre Dame Press, 1967) pp. 167, 169–174. © 1965 by D. C. Watt. Reprinted by permission of the publisher.

tions was exerted after the Godesberg meeting between Hitler and Chamberlain, and the latter's discovery of German intransigence. . . .

27 September was the critical day. That day the Cabinet heard the Dominions' views in detail, together with a telegram from Lyons, the Australian premier. Although Duff Cooper, the most European-minded of the Cabinet, argued strongly against their acceptance, stigmatizing them as unrepresentative of the real feeling in the Dominions, his views were not borne out by the anxieties of the High Commissioners. . . .

It is clear on the evidence available that had the British Government pursued a course animated by other sentiments than those which inspired them, they would have lost the backing of South Africa, have found Australia divided and unhappy and might well have put the Canadian Government in a very difficult position; and that they had considerable advance warning of this from the Dominions High Commissioners in London, and the Dominions Governments. The advance warning of the attitude of the Dominions given at the Imperial Conference of 1937, reiterated by the Dominions High Commissioners after the occupation of Austria, is of great importance in explaining the rigidity of the British determination not to become involved in central Europe, expressed in the combination of extreme pressure on Beneš to make concessions to the demands of the Sudeten Germans, and evasiveness whenever Beneš tried to extract some assurance of Western support with which to buttress himself in making such concessions against Czech public opinion.

The knowledge of Dominions opposition to the idea of a war over Czechoslovakia is, of course, only one of the factors which went to make up the policy of appeasement which reached its culmination at Munich. There were other equally important factors in the general weakness of the British position when faced with the possibility of war, which Chamberlain and Halifax felt so strongly. The moral strength of the German nationalist case against Versailles, if judged, as they came to judge it, by that curious combination of power-political principles and Wilsonian morality which ruled international politics between the wars, and their consciousness of British military weakness were possibly more important. Most important perhaps, given these considerations, was their consciousness of the lost opportunities of 1930–36, the opportunities of reaching agreement with Hitler's predecessors, the opportunities of maintaining a Franco-Italian front against Hitler, the opportunities of tying him down with new pacts which he himself had negotiated, opportunities which French opposition, the state of British public opinion and, it should be added, Hitler's own evasiveness had denied them. All of this added up to the conviction that in 1938 they were in no state to go to war, and that to maintain Czech rule over the Sudetens until a peace conference would provide the opportunity of returning them to Germany, was no cause on which to fight one.

J. W. Wheeler-Bennett

THE DRAMA OF MUNICH

Wheeler-Bennett's work on Munich might be classified as either a contemporary or a historical study. In fact it is both, for he was an analyst and reporter of international affairs beginning in 1924 when he founded the *Bulletin of International News,* a publication of the Royal Institute of International Affairs with which he was long associated, and he was also able to use the documents and memoirs that had been published by the time he wrote his book on Munich. Among the best-known of his other publications are *Wooden Titan: Hindenburg, Brest-Litovsk: the Forgotten Peace,* and *Nemesis of Power: the German Army and Politics.* The excerpts here reprinted are but highlights of his full-length study of Munich and its consequences; they emphasize the significance of Berchtesgaden, and judiciously appraise the meaning of Munich. Would you conclude from these excerpts that Munich was the result of bad judgment (a blunder) or of weakness in the character of British and French leadership?

THE Berchtesgaden visit is, in many respects, of greater historical importance than the Munich Conference itself; it set in motion a procession of events to which Munich was the tragic climax and the inevitable sequel. For, once direct appeasement had been begun on the basis of personal contact, it was almost impossible to stop the process without the certainty of war. From then on the issue depended on a time-table, a schedule of evacuations and frontier delimitations, on neither of which, once the main principle of surrender had been accepted, would it have been possible to have obtained full public support for war.

Before Mr. Chamberlain went to Berchtesgaden he had believed that Germany had not really intended to go as far as to risk war in order to attain her ambitions, but his meeting with the Führer convinced him that this risk would not only be taken, but taken immediately if Hitler's demands were not granted. "I have no doubt whatever," Mr. Chamberlain later told the Commons, "that my visit alone prevented an invasion, for which everything was ready." This, of course, was not entirely true, since the earliest date for the X-Day of "Operation Green" was September 30, and at no time did Hitler deviate from this time-table. But Mr. Chamberlain had carried away an accurate impression of the Führer's inflexible determination to march into the Sudetenland, and it was clear to him that, if peace were to be preserved, Hitler's demands on Czechoslovakia must be granted; and once this principle had been accepted, it seemed virtually impossible to go to war later over ways and means. The historic moment of decision, therefore, was at Berchtesgaden, and, though the subsequent tide of events might ebb and flow, the ultimate outcome was inevitable.

For France the decision which Mr. Chamberlain took at Berchtesgaden, and which MM. Daladier and Bonnet ratified in London, was even more vital. By her agreement to abandon Czechoslovakia France destroyed her own military se-

From *Munich: Prologue to Tragedy* by J. W. Wheeler-Bennett, pp. 116–118, 164–167, 434–435, by permission of Duell, Sloan, and Pearce, affiliate of Meredith Press. Copyright 1948 by John W. Wheeler-Bennett.

curity, but she also abdicated her right to be considered a Great Power and began that fatal descent which ended in the Avernus of Vichy, and on which Munich was but a milestone.

The Berchtesgaden meeting was also important for Hitler. Though he had been persistently certain that Britain, and therefore France, would not fight for the Sudetenland—he was so sure that he had only moved five extra divisions to supplement the normal defence force on the Western Frontier—and was quite undeterred by Mr. Chamberlain's debating point on the differentiation between "threats" and "warnings," he received impressions during his conversations with the Prime Minister which gave additional confirmation to his convictions. These impressions the Führer passed on to his uncertain Southern ally—and to good effect. It was not until after the Berchtesgaden meeting had convinced the Italian Government of the weakness of the Western democracies that Mussolini began his series of speeches in the leading cities of Italy (September 18–26) in which he consistently intimated that, in the event of war, Italy would support her Axis partner.

The Führer, moreover, was materially aided by the fact that, by allowing the German proposals to be submitted to Prague as the "Anglo-French Plan," the British and French Governments had automatically made themselves to some degree the accomplices of Hitler in the eyes of the world. Had the German ultimatum been transmitted—as was later the case after Godesberg—as a purely German document, it would still have been open to both Governments to give such advice, or apply such pressure, to the Czechs as they might see fit in order to ensure its acceptance, and their hands would have been a good deal cleaner. As it was, Britain and France allowed themselves to appear before world public opinion as Hitler's willing bailiffs.

*   *   *

[On September 27, Chamberlain reverted to the idea of a four-power conference with a Czech representative present that he had proposed to Masaryk on September 25.]

The Prime Minister telephoned to Paris. M. Daladier and M. Bonnet were now delighted with the idea—M. Bonnet especially so. The idea of a Four-Power Conference had been discussed in the Chamber of Deputies that afternoon, where M. Louis-Oscar Frossard had warmly advocated it. As a result of these conversations both Mr. Chamberlain and M. Bonnet sent messages to the Duce urging him to support the proposal, and the Prime Minister at once telegraphed a reply to Hitler.

He was ready, he said, to come to Berlin at once to discuss arrangements for the transfer of the Sudeten Territory with the Führer and a representative of the Czechoslovak Government, and with those of France and Italy, if Hitler so desired. "I feel convinced we could reach agreement in a week," he wrote, and added: "I cannot believe that you will take responsibility of starting a world war which may end civilization for the sake of a few days' delay in settling this long-standing problem."

But Mr. Chamberlain had reckoned without Georges Bonnet, and Georges Bonnet was wedded to the twin thought that there should be no war and that Hitler should get what he wanted. The French Foreign Minister had already that day denied all knowledge of the British Foreign Office communiqué of September 26 pledging France, Britain and Russia to support Czechoslovakia, and he had authorized the Agence Havas to deny categorically the statement that a general mobilization had been ordered in Germany for 2 P.M. on September 28. He was doing his best to keep France anaesthetized. Now while Mr. Chamberlain was sending messages to the Führer and the Duce, M. Bonnet telegraphed his own explicit instructions to the French Ambassador in Berlin.

The instructions were of such a nature that when M. François-Poncet received them at an early hour on the morning of September 28 he could not at first believe his eyes, and in any case he had some difficulty in gaining access to the Führer. Ironically enough it was only through the intervention of Sir Nevile Henderson and Göring that he was received by Hitler at all. However, he finally gained audience at 11.15 A.M. and the Führer, when he had read his message, talked with him for an hour "in altogether a different tone," as M. François-Poncet afterwards said, "from that which he had used previously with my British colleague." The interview was interrupted at 11.40 for a hurried conversation between Hitler and the Italian Ambassador, who had arrived with an appeal from Mussolini for a stay of twenty-four hours in the German mobilization. When he returned, Hitler said to Poncet: "I cannot say no to your suggestion. I will give you a written answer this afternoon."

Well might the Führer acquiesce in the suggestion which M. François-Poncet had brought him, for it was no less than a wholesale surrender on the part of France. M. Bonnet's proposals were ostensibly intended to be presented as a last-minute effort to placate Hitler in the event of his rejection of the British proposals, which had been already received by President Beneš and were at that moment still reposing in Sir Nevile Henderson's brief-case. The Führer, therefore, received the French offer before he had read the British, and it was considerably more generous.

Where Mr. Chamberlain had offered one zone, M. Bonnet offered three, all of which were to be occupied on October 1, though it was stipulated that the Czechs must retain their fortifications. There was, however, an air about the Note which seemed to indicate that even this did not represent the last word in French amenability and that, provided that Hitler did not go to war, further pressure might be brought upon Prague to accept further demands if they were forthcoming. It was the climax of the betrayal of Czechoslovakia, seeming to justify the bitter comment of an English author, written years before, that "France, among a multitude of virtues, has one vice, unpardonable to Northern men: she turns from a fallen friend."

When Sir Nevile Henderson arrived with Mr. Chamberlain's letter at 12.15, Hitler greeted him with the news that "at the request of my great friend and ally, Mussolini," the German general mobilization had been postponed for twenty-four hours. But he would not agree to send a reply to the letter until he had further consulted the Duce. However, the Führer was once again interrupted by the indefatigable Signor Attolico, this time in order to bring Mussolini's enthusiastic endorsement of the proposal for a Four-Power Conference. After this it was all plain sailing, and by lunch-time the invitations to Munich had been despatched.

In reality, however, the whole thing had been settled well before Mr. Chamberlain's letter was even placed in the hands of the Führer, and the principal factors in assuring a "peaceful settlement" had not been the faint-heartedness of Mussolini; nor the opposition of the German General Staff; nor the last-minute qualms of Göring; nor the appeals of President Roosevelt; nor even the mobilization of the British Fleet: the principal factors were the Laodicean policy of Britain and the ignoble conduct of France.

Hitler had neither "climbed down" nor "lost face." He had had everything he wanted handed to him on a silver salver. In postponing mobilization for twenty-four hours, he had given away nothing, since the threat of it remained suspended like a Damoclean sword during the ensuing discussions, and in any case the striking force was already on the Czech frontier. He would get his military occupation of the Sudetenland none the less. The Czechs would be crushed and "that Beneš" would be humbled. And the Führer's intelligence told him, moreover, that once the war tension in Britain and France had been relaxed it would be a very difficult task to persuade the peoples of those countries again to screw their courage to the sticking-place and resign themselves once more to the prospect of war.

*   *   *

The apologists for Munich cannot have it both ways. Either Britain was so ill-armed and undefended that she was, with great reluctance, forced to a certain course of action in order to ensure peace, or else she *was* in a position to fight, and, of her own free will, chose not to do so. In neither case is there cause for self-approbation, but there is less ground for contrition in the first than the second. It may be true that we could not "stand up to Hitler and damn the consequences," but if so we should not be proud of it.

Moreover, it must not be forgotten that the whole basis of the defence of Munich shifted midway between October 1938 and March 1939. The original argument of Mr. Chamberlain, Sir John Simon, Sir Samuel Hoare, and Sir Thomas Inskip was that the Prime Minister had saved the world from war and had brought back "Peace for Our Time." Later, however, when the international situation began to deteriorate, the Munich Agreement began to be hailed by its supporters not so much as a great act of statesmanship which had preserved anew the palladium of peace, as an astute act of diplomacy by which Britain had "bought time" in order to complete her rearmament and build up her defences. Of this last argument there was no sign in October 1938, and, in any case, whichever claim is made for Munich, it was a failure.

Henri Noguères

FRENCH DIPLOMATIC FAILURE

A journalist who had already begun his career on the Socialist newspaper *Populaire* two years before Munich, Henri Noguères has continued since the Second World War to edit and write for newspapers and periodicals and for radio and television. He has also published historical studies ranging over topics from the 16th to the 20th century. The excerpts below from his work on Munich omit many of the details of his accusations against Bonnet and the French government, but give the substance of his analysis of the "errors" that he believes they made. Does he go farther than Pertinax, for example, and accuse Bonnet of a determination to give Germany a free hand in the East? Or does he charge him merely with lacking the will to fight? Incidentally, why does he think Munich was not a necessity?

N O one will deny that in entrusting Georges Bonnet with Paul-Boncour's post [foreign minister], Daladier had certainly chosen a man whose personal qualities would arouse violent reactions; and that, furthermore, as much in liberal right-wing circles in France and abroad as among the people who were called "left-wingers."

GENERAL GAMELIN: M. Georges Bonnet became foreign minister. In my opinion this last appointment was exceedingly unfortunate, for he never stopped playing an equivocal part . . . He was a very intelligent man, but he had no deep convictions, and it might even be said no morals. In everything he saw his own immediate personal interest alone, and he had a natural taste for intrigue. On several occasions I was able to establish that one could never trust what he said. . . .

JEAN ZAY, THE MINISTER OF EDUCATION: The intention of abandoning Czechoslovakia and Poland if they were attacked, that is to say, of repudiating the solemn engagements undertaken by all our governments since 1920, and the determination to leave Germany completely free to do as she wished in the east and in central Eur-

ope dated from long before the crises of September. It was an already-established and thoroughly-considered basic attitude, and its chief exponent inside Daladier's ministry was the foreign minister himself, M. Georges Bonnet. Perhaps he would not be blamed for it if he had announced it openly. The cabinet would have made its choice. But he pursued this scheme in a secret manner, at the same time making a display of ostensible adherence to the official line of conduct of the government of which he was a member.

WINSTON CHURCHILL: Many of us had the sensation that Bonnet represented the quintessence of defeatism, and that all his clever verbal manoeuvres had the aim of "peace at any price."

EDUARD BENES: Bonnet's reputation was that of a gambler and an unblushing and shameless grafter for whom all roads were good so long as they led to the place he wished to reach. As a minister he sent instructions by telegram or letter that were in line with the government's official declarations. At the same time he gave diametrically opposite orders by word of mouth. He was a priori against any diplomatic or military resistance to Hitler's expansionism. What he would have preferred to anything

From Henri Noguères, *Munich: "Peace for our time,"* tr. by Patrick O'Brian (New York: McGraw-Hill Book Company, 1965), pp. 44–46, 358–363, 371–374, 376–382, 384–390. French edition © 1963 by Robert Laffont, Paris; English translation © 1965 by George Weidenfeld and Nicolson Ltd. Reprinted by permission.

was an armed struggle between the Nazis and the Bolsheviks.

What were the reasons that had induced Daladier, apart from purely political considerations, to pick Georges Bonnet rather than some other member of parliament of the same group?

"I chose M Georges Bonnet as foreign minister," said Daladier, "because in 1932 he had presided over the Stresa conference on the economic reconstruction of central Europe and because when he had been appointed ambassador to Washington by Léon Blum's government he had been able to gain the undoubted esteem of President Roosevelt, Sumner Welles, the assistant Secretary of State, and the political circles, as well as a fortunate influence over them.
"In his second government Léon Blum invited him to be ambassador a second time. The choice of M Bonnet was very favourably commented upon in the foreign papers, particularly those of America and England and Soviet Russia too."

If that is indeed what Daladier thought of his foreign minister, what was Bonnet's opinion of his political chief?
    A few days after his arrival at the Quai d'Orsay Georges Bonnet asked Pierre Lazareff, the editor of *Paris-Soir*, to luncheon at Carton's, in the Place de la Madeleine. Lazareff noted down the gist of his conversation with the new foreign minister, particularly what Bonnet said to him about Daladier.

A strange man, Daladier; difficult to know. If he is popular with the army it is because he has always backed up the general staff, letting them do what they like and never going against their plans. If he is accepted by the Socialists and the right wing it is because both the one set and the other are out of power by reason of the parliamentary majority, and both suppose that they can govern through him, for he is a hesitant man and susceptible to influence. Besides, Daladier is clever enough to make both hope that he will indeed govern with them. Furthermore, Daladier has the appearance of a strong man. He will be very good at giving the country (forgetful of the bad days) the impression that France herself is strong. As we are weak, what I for my part fear most is that although this country may be taken in, Hitler will not . . .

As for his policy, Georges Bonnet defined it for his companion; and it cannot be said that he was not frank.

Don't let us go in for heroism; we are not up to it. . . . The English will not follow us. . . . As foreign minister I am determined to play my part fully, and it consists of finding a solution before the minister of war has to take one. France can no longer allow herself a blood-letting like that of 1914. Our population figures are going down every day. And finally the Front Populaire has reduced the country to such a state that it must get ready for a sensible convalescence —a rash movement might be fatal.

Where Czechoslovakia was concerned, therefore, Georges Bonnet showed himself reticent to say the least. He chose to remember only those parts of Chamberlain's declarations that allowed reserves on Great Britain's part to be detected, and he finished by saying,

When you state that you are not sure that you will fight, but that "perhaps for all that" you may fight, believe me, a man like Hitler understands that he is simply being asked not to act in such a way that we shall be forced to fight him. Moreover, I think this English policy both intelligent and wise.

                    *   *   *

. . . Public opinion has long since condemned Munich and the spirit of Munich.
    Is this condemnation just? Is there to be no appeal from it?
    It is for the reader, who has all the evidence before him, to decide.
    Yet without encroaching upon this decision or trying to suggest the reasons that should be adduced, we think it allowable to draw up a balance-sheet, by way of conclusion. This is all the easier today, since a quarter of a century has passed since Munich, and the strong feelings of the time, although they may not have died quite away, are henceforward confined to the justifications of the parts they played by the last of those who took a leading role at the conference. . . .
    To begin with we must go back to a short analysis of the legal situation as it was in the first place, since it was the ob-

ligations that her allies undertook with regard to Czechoslovakia that were at the origin of the international tension which culminated in Munich.

In 1938 Czechoslovakia's security and the integrity of her boundaries were guaranteed by international agreements. France had signed one of these. The USSR for its part had consented to another; but this contained a suspensive clause which laid down that the agreement should be operative only after the Franco-Czechoslovak treaty should have come into effect. People have too often forgotten to point out that this suspensive clause was only inserted into the Russo-Czechoslovak pact in 1935 *at the express request of the French government,* justifiably anxious to avoid a position in which Russia could set off a war by her own motion.

France had therefore reserved to herself the right to be the first, and practically the sole, judge of when these obligations that had been undertaken by herself and the USSR should have to be fulfilled. This right of selecting the proper moment was all the more readily accepted by the leaders of the Czechoslovak Republic since it was to be exercised by France, a country whose international prestige was then based upon a long and splendid tradition of scrupulous respect for obligation assumed, for the given word, and for the signature at the bottom of a contract. . . .

However, as the months went by, and the Nazi threat to Czechoslovakia became clearer and with it the risk of war greater, a current of opinion in France that favoured a "restrictive interpretation" of the Franco-Czechoslovak pact came into being and increased in strength. This did not happen all at once. On February 26, 1938, Yvon Delbos, the foreign minister, stated in parliament that "France's engagements towards Czechoslovakia would be faithfully fulfilled in case of need." The next day the premier, Camille Chautemps, confirmed this.

A few weeks later, on March 14, immediately after the Anschluss, Paul-Boncour, who had just succeeded Delbos at the Quai d'Orsay, in his turn made the same statement.

But in the foreign affairs committee of the Chamber P.-E. Flandin reproached Paul-Boncour for taking up this attitude, asserting that "the collapse of the treaty of Locarno, to which our last treaty with Czechoslovakia was bound, it being signed the same day and as one of its consequences, rendered the latter null and void."

Shortly afterwards Joseph Barthélémy expressed the same point of view in his well-known article in *Le Temps,* doing his utmost to provide it with a juridical basis. . . .

Professor René Cassin demolished these juridical excuses as early as August, 1938, by showing that if Czechoslovakia owed France assistance in the event of Germany's violating the Rhineland pact or the Franco-German arbitration treaty, then France was bound to come to the help of Czechoslovakia in the event of the violation of the arbitration convention between Germany and Czechoslovakia, which was still in force. And René Cassin ended, "The nations must be warned against the persuasion that even the plainest of treaties is not binding once the execution of it entails certain risks. Civilization can continue to exist only if treaties are respected."

Nevertheless Flandin's and Barthélémy's thesis gained many adherents. . . . There were ministers within Daladier's government who shared this point of view: on September 13 Anatole de Monzie also made a laborious juridical survey, by which he established that in the event of a German attack upon Czechoslovakia, at the most France would be required (and only after the League of Nations had intervened) to take economic sanctions against Germany. Since the Abyssinian affair everyone knew what "economic sanctions" amounted to.

In justice it must be said that neither Daladier nor even Georges Bonnet openly adopted this argument during the first six months of the German-Czechoslovak crisis, that is to say, from the Anschluss to Munich.

In London Daladier even went so far as to emphasize the engagements undertaken by France. And in his speech at La Pointe de Grave Bonnet, alluding to the

Czechoslovak affair directly, said, "In any event France will remain faithful to the obligations she has contracted.". . .

There was an ever-increasing disparity between their words and their deeds, for while they spoke of the obligations that France had undertaken they never stopped acting in such a manner that they would not have to fulfil them. They carried on this course of action with remarkable perseverance, particularly in their attempts at causing it to be understood that it was impossible for France to intervene physically unless she was assured of British support; yet Great Britain was not bound to Czechoslovakia by any pact of the nature of the Franco-Czechoslovak treaty of 1925.

However, the French government were basing themselves upon the attitude taken up by the British when, on September 20, they brought pressure to bear on the Czechoslovak government to induce them to accept a "Franco-British plan" that reiterated all the requirements that Hitler had laid down at Berchtesgaden on September 15. And the only way in which this pressure could be made effective was by the threat of not keeping the promises that had been made.

And when, after the Godesberg ultimatum, Great Britain nevertheless agreed at last that she might come in on the French side (though she was not obliged to do so), the Quai d'Orsay set the most discreditable machinery in motion to try to conceal this change of front from French public opinion. As a last resource Georges Bonnet's people even went so far as to accuse what others considered a victory for French diplomacy of being a forgery.

The responsibility for this development of French policy, for this withdrawal from the possible consequences of engagements undertaken, must of course fall primarily upon the government. Yet one must not underestimate the part played, both in France and England, by a public opinion that carried fear of war to the point of mass cowardice.

It is true that public opinion, particularly in times of extreme tension, can be influenced. What is more, it can be misled.

"People of France, you are being deceived!" proclaimed Flandin in his poster of September 28. And as we have seen he then, with virtuous indignation, denounced "the hidden forces that have set cunning machinery in motion to make war inevitable."

It can scarcely be denied that hidden forces did operate and that cunning machinery was set in motion. Yet one has but to leaf through the files of the main daily and weekly papers to see that the pressure exerted on public opinion was brought to bear by the "peace at any price" party and not by the "war party."

*   *   *

The hysterical crowds that welcomed Daladier at Le Bourget and Chamberlain at Heston on September 30 did not regard the Munich agreement as a last resource, a makeshift.

Yet apart from the paid agents of the fifth column none of those who defended the Munich agreement immediately after its signature, nor any of those far fewer people who continued to defend it later, claimed to see it as anything but a lesser evil.

The defenders of Munich and of the "Munich spirit" made use of the doctrine that was Hitler's golden rule, the reason for his success and for his fall: they attributed to the provisionally peaceful settlement that was reached on September 29, 1938, one essential "virtue," that of being realistic.

Clearly when it was a question of Munich it was easier to see it as a display of realism rather than the application of those moral rules that give both the nations and the private persons who observe them a clear conscience.

It would be tempting to enter into a discourse upon the merits of political realism and to inquire how far it absolves a nation from very dishonourable conduct; but this is not the place to do so. . . . Nevertheless, since these are important factors in the balance-sheet of Munich, we must look for the arguments upon which those who still look upon realism as the justification for the agreement can base themselves.

These arguments fall into three categories, and they may be objectively summarized thus:

1. It was necessary to see that peace was kept in September 1938 because of the attitude of the USSR, which, though Czechoslovakia's ally, produced nothing but good advice and did nothing to overcome the diplomatic obstacles to an eventual military intervention.

2. The proportion of the opposing forces, both in central Europe and in a possible western theatre of operations, was so favourable to the Axis in September 1938 that it was impossible for France, even if it were granted that England would come in on her side, to engage in a conflict.

3. Finally, the Munich peace, however precarious it may have been, did provide the democracies with a respite that allowed them to alter this proportion so that it was to their advantage.

Each of these three points, diplomatic isolation, military weakness and respite, deserves to be looked into and discussed.

The Soviet Union, allied with France since the signature of the Franco-Soviet pact of May 2, 1935, which was negotiated by Laval, and with Czechoslovakia by the terms of the Russo-Czechoslovak treaty concluded a fortnight later on May 16, was the only counterpoise in eastern Europe that could, by opening an eastern front, make Hitler hesitate.

It still had to be known whether on the one hand the USSR would honour its signature in the event of open conflict and come in on the side of its allies, and on the other whether the Red Army would, in spite of the absence of a common frontier between Czechoslovakia and Russia, be physically capable of intervening.

According to Georges Bonnet and Daladier the reply to the first question was, in a theoretical and grudging manner, affirmative; but there was no possible doubt that the answer to the second was negative. In other words Russia was all the freer in declaring herself ready to stand by her engagements since she was sure of having a valid excuse for not having to keep them.

This interpretation is based on the negative result of a series of approaches undertaken by French diplomats, and even by Georges Bonnet in person on several occasions, particularly behind the scenes at the League of Nations—approaches to the Rumanians and Poles to ask them to let the Red Army go through their territories in the event of a German aggression against Czechoslovakia.

It is certain that these démarches took place. Nor is there any question that they met with a flat refusal on the part of Beck or his colleagues and with a more delicately shaded refusal from Comnenus.

But it is far less evident that the USSR would have used these difficulties as a pretext if Czechoslovakia had been attacked.

In point of fact the Western powers, and more particularly Chamberlain and his personal advisers in England and Bonnet and his "pacifist" associates in France, had only one fear—that of finding themselves engaged in a European war against Nazi Germany and fascist Italy, the two countries "of order," and on the same side as Bolshevik Russia, the centre of disorder and subversion. What is more the example of the Spanish war was there before their eyes, to increase their dread; they could not feel sympathy with the "reds," supported by Moscow. How could they contemplate becoming in their turn part of the "red" camp?

In order to get rid of this untimely and compromising alliance it was necessary to prove, at any cost, that the USSR had very little desire to keep its international engagements, and could not do so, in any case. And this, by the bye, at the very moment France, while repeating solemn assurances that she should remain faithful to her own obligations, was getting ready not to keep them.

No doubt the French government hoped that by keeping systematically in step with Great Britain (who was in no way bound to Czechoslovakia) and by taking care not to reply to the Soviet offers of military co-operation they would discourage the Russians. . . . So Bonnet stubbornly kept to the letter as far as the "technical" possibilities of a Russian intervention were concerned, and pretended to deplore Soviet formalism. And in the same way Daladier, in the matter of a possible appeal to the League, merely decried the "ramshackle machinery of Geneva," just as Hitler and Mussolini did.

It is pleasant to hear another note in a statement upon these two basic aspects of Franco-Soviet relations in 1938. Coulondre, the French ambassador in Moscow, gives particularly exact information on the Russian military preparations in liaison with the Czechoslovaks which proves that they genuinely intended to intervene. Speaking of the démarches undertaken in Moscow by Zdenek Fierlinger, the head of the Czechoslovak diplomatic mission, he writes,

He has obtained the immediate delivery of sixty bombers. Twenty have already landed at the airfield of Uggorod in Slovakia. It is thus proved that Russian planes can land in the less immediately threatened part of the country. On their side the Russians have laid out a great airfield at Vinnitza, considerably nearer the frontier west of Kiev. The Uggorod airfield, where the work had to be held up because of a German press campaign, is not yet finished and it still has to be supplied with the spare parts and petrol storage needed for the Soviet planes.

Furthermore, on September 15 the Rumanian government gave up their opposition to having their territory flown over and informed Thierry, the French minister in Bucarest. Shortly after General Delmas, the French military attaché in Rumania, noticed a significant incident: a Soviet plane made a forced landing on a Rumanian airfield and when it was repaired it was allowed to fly on to Czechoslovakia. At the time of Munich, therefore, it was possible to count roughly two hundred Soviet aeroplanes delivered to Czechoslovak airfields. . . .

But the more evident the determination of the Russians became, the stronger grew Georges Bonnet's reserve. How could it have been otherwise, once the French foreign minister had finally made up his mind to the policy of appeasement?

Later, and the paradox was only apparent, he openly complained that France was reduced to defending Czechoslovakia by herself (which led him to do nothing of the kind out of "realism") while at the same time he was using every way of hiding the firmness of the Soviets and the stiffening of the British attitude from French public opinion.

The business of the Foreign Office communiqué of September 26 illustrates this duplicity: not only was the communiqué, which pointed out the support given to France by Great Britain and the USSR, at once described as a forgery, but the dispatches that confirmed its official origin mysteriously vanished as soon as they reached the Quai d'Orsay, and the authenticity of the document was finally acknowledged only on September 30—after Munich.

This fear of seeing the Russians concerning themselves with the Czechoslovak affair and upsetting the contemplated "peaceful" settlement induced Daladier and Bonnet to agree that the Munich conference should be held without the USSR, although Russia was France's ally.

Yet some days before Russia had let it be known that she would agree to be represented at a conference of the great powers and the states concerned: Litvinov had stated this at Geneva to Mr. Butler, the Under-Secretary of State at the Foreign Office, and Lord De La Warr, the Lord Privy Seal, who had asked him the question in the presence of Maisky, the Soviet ambassador in London.

This "overlooking" of Russia at the time of Munich is severely criticized by so experienced a diplomat as Coulondre.

"Certain documents," he says, "particularly a note taken by Schmundt, the Chancellor's aide-de-camp, lead one to think that the allies might perhaps still have been able to deal with the situation immediately before Munich if they had had the courage and the common sense to insist that the USSR and Czechoslovakia should take part in the conference.

"By Munich itself France and Great Britain had lost the essential part of the game.

Yet at least with a little energy they might have secured that the amputation of the Sudetenland should take place in less disadvantageous conditions, and above all that the remaining Czechoslovak territory should be guaranteed without reserves or conditions by the four signatory powers. Czechoslovakia would have been mutilated and neutralized, but not sacrificed.

"By the end of the summer of 1938 the peace-loving powers could scarcely avoid going to Munich. The mistake was to go there without Russia and with the 'Munich spirit.'"

The American ambassador in Moscow, in 1938, Davies, was one of the first to foresee the dramatic consequences of this mistake. On January 18, 1939, that is to say seven months before the signature of the German-Soviet pact, Davies wrote to Harry Hopkins:

"Chamberlain's policy, which is pushing Italy, Poland and Hungary into Hitler's arms, may end by disgusting the Soviets to such a degree that it will induce Russia to come to an economic agreement and a political truce with Hitler. This is not beyond the range of possibility nor even of probability—for ten years it was a fact." And Davies added, "The reactionaries in England and France will presently, in their despair, beg for the Soviets' support, but perhaps it will be too late, if between now and then the Soviets grow utterly disgusted by their attitude." . . .

So far from being a voluntary withdrawal, as Georges Bonnet would have it, Russia's diplomatic isolation at the time of Munich was in fact the result of the Western powers' systematic mistrust and of those "useless obstacles" that Churchill denounced in his speech at Manchester.

This mistrust and these obstacles are to be found again in another field, and one no less important—that of military co-operation.

Georges Bonnet has stuffed his brief with evidence to prove that on several occasions he did question the Russians as to what they could do to intervene in the event of a German attack upon Czechoslovakia. But each time the French foreign minister contented himself with hearing the reply he expected, that is to say, that the crossing of Poland or Rumania by the Red Army would set delicate diplomatic problems.

Yet there was a way of getting over, or getting round, this obstacle in procedure: it was to go straight to the concrete aspect of things and to set the general staffs (which would have to carry out the operations, after all) the task of planning a joint strategy and of comparing the ends to be achieved with the means at their disposal. It is easy to guess the objection: what would be the point of staff-talks, since the Russians could not bring a single soldier into the field?

It may seem an attractive argument for a moment, but it will not bear examination. In the first place it should be observed that talks of this kind had been carried on with the British, although their contribution to a possible European campaign could only be a token force, and that for a long while. And then again it is not true to say that even if the passage of Russian troops through Rumania or Poland were deliberately excluded, direct Soviet military assistance to Czechoslovakia would necessarily have been trifling. In the field of aviation alone Russian intervention would have been enough to take the control of the air from the Luftwaffe—to say nothing of the effect on the German population of raids as reprisals for the bombing of Czech towns.

Besides, why was Georges Bonnet so insistent that the Soviet intervention could only come about by means of a passage through Rumania or Poland, arranged on a "friendly basis"?

Surely in such a case it was the general staffs' duty to seek and find alternative solutions—for example, that diversion in East Prussia which, as it later appeared, was for a long while the chief anxiety of the German general staff. And did not the Quai d'Orsay also know that Poland was ready to combine with Germany in the event of an attack upon Czechoslovakia, and that in this event Russia intended to go into action against Poland—without asking for her authorization?

Lastly, the mere fact of beginning talks of this kind would have given a clearer view of the real intentions of our possible partner and at the same time it would, in case of need, have made it possible to overcome any remaining reserves by making use of the soldiers to overcome the civilians.

But all this would have called for a desire to act on the part of the French leaders (and of the British, if in the event they had chosen to come in), and not the a priori exclusion of any possibility of a clash.

Georges Bonnet has assumed the task of proving that France was alone in meaning to go as far as war in order to stand by her engagements. In fact there were others, that is to say, Czechoslovakia and the USSR, who considered this risk. But he, on the contrary, so completely excluded it that he told Daladier of his intention to resign if a war should break out over the Czechoslovak affair.

Furthermore it was because he had taken his decision and made his choice that he never stopped minimizing the desire to intervene on the part of France's possible partners or their possibilities of doing so....

Yet Russia's military potentialities were not trifling. To refuse contacts that would have allowed the beginning of a fruitful collaboration between the general staff of the Red Army and those of the Western powers could only mean that in Paris there was a determination to put up with all Hitler's exigencies in advance and to avoid war at all costs.

In the field of aviation—that which was worrying the French general staff most since General Vuillemin's depressing trip to Germany—Russia alone possessed an air force that was enough to outmatch the Luftwaffe. As Daladier said on several occasions, the Russian air force was the most numerous in Europe. But in addition to this, since the spring of 1938 the Soviet government had put forty-five motorized divisions on a war footing and had gathered them all on her western frontier.

For their part the Czechoslovaks amounted to an important military force in central Europe. The responsibility for this estimate again falls upon Daladier: "The mobilized Czech army represented a considerable force, well-equipped and well-officered, of thirty-five divisions. Its fortifications were partially outflanked by the annexation of Austria. But in spite of that the army intelligence reckoned the Czech resistance at one month at the least 'on condition that she should have Germany alone to deal with.'"

Furthermore the necessary steps had been taken, immediately after the Anschluss, to re-order the Czechoslovak troop dispositions in the light of this new situation. . . . As for the Czechoslovak air force ("excellent," according to Daladier), it was, as the head of the French military mission points out, quite remarkably powerful. . . .

Germany did dispose of a certain superiority in the eastern theatre of operations in the case of an attack upon Czechoslovakia and before any Russian intervention, for she had more than forty divisions, including a fairly high proportion of armoured units.

Yet this superiority was not so great that the "four days" that Hitler gave for the Czechoslovak army's resistance were to be taken seriously. And even the estimate of a month made by the French army intelligence did not by any means correspond with the pessimistic forecast of the German general staff. . . .

And Hitler himself said, "What we were able to see of the military strength of the Czechoslovaks greatly disturbed us; we had run a serious danger."

If the relative strength of the opposing forces in the eastern theatre in September 1938 made the German generals doubtful about the outcome of a war, the situation in the west, on the French frontier, filled them with dismay.

It was no longer a matter of calculating the comparative inadequacy of their superiority in numbers: for while the mobilized French army could range close on a hundred divisions against Germany and Italy, the commander-in-chief appointed to the western theatre, General Wilhelm Adam, had only twelve at his disposal, and of those, as we have seen, only five were regular divisions; and his strength in the air was reduced to this barest minimum, since the mass of the German air force was assigned to Operation Green. As for the Siegfried line fortifications they were as yet nothing more than "a building-site," as Jodl put it, not only devoid of military value, but of such a kind that they would in fact hinder the defenders in their task.

In these conditions it was of little consequence that Great Britain should not, for a fairly long time, be able to send more than a single army corps to the continent.

It is wholly understandable that the German generals, all the German generals without exception, were opposed to the war....

It is even true, and Daladier points it out with great pride, that after the signature of the Munich agreement Hitler was far from pleased. Was he displeased, because, as he said to Schacht, he had missed making his entry into Prague, although this was only put off until later? No doubt he was. But above all he was displeased at the sight of the German people so openly showing their peaceful feelings.

At all events there was one point upon which Hitler had no room for displeasure —the famous "respite" that Munich granted peace. For he knew better than anyone that he would be not only the first but indeed the only person to benefit from this respite. Yet this is the argument, the third in the list, that is most often advanced by those who defend the Munich agreement.

There is almost no point in demolishing it, because it is known, alas, how much in favour of the Western powers was the balance of strength in September 1938, and it is known how the war that broke out after a year of respite did in fact develop. Nevertheless, since it is a factor in the balance-sheet, we must show the consequences of this year that was "gained." It does not appear that anyone goes so far as to claim that the French and the English were able, on the moral plane, to derive any sort of advantage from Munich, particularly when it was seen in perspective: loss of prestige and an uneasy conscience—that was how the result of the meeting of September 1938 may be summarized as far as this aspect is concerned.

On the military plane, which is said to be that upon which the "respite" was worth most, what the Allies lost in that year was incalculably great....

Finally, and there is no doubt that this was far from the least grave of the consequences of this "pause for thought," Davies's clear-sighted and pessimistic forecast was to be proved true.

Before Munich, when she had proposed staff-talks, and at the time of Munich, when she saw her ally France taking part without her in a conference that was to determine the balance of power in Europe, Russia could see that in the mind of the French government the Franco-Soviet pact was henceforward considered a dead letter.

After Munich the USSR had only to observe the repeated violations of the agreement and France's passive conduct to be sure that Bonnet and Daladier would from then on leave Hitler "a free hand in the east." ...

So in the end we are obliged to agree with Churchill's summing up. "For all the above reasons, the year's breathing-space said to have been 'gained' by Munich left Britain and France in a much worse position compared with Hitler's Germany than they had been at the Munich crisis."

It is impossible to give a clearer definition of what was—as this balance-sheet has just shown and as the subsequent events were to prove—one of the most wretched of diplomatic failures.

Yet it would be wrong, as we recall the facts in the perspective of history, and with the assurance of hindsight, to forget that in September 1938, virtually the entire population of France, with a greater or lesser degree of thoughtless exuberance, restraint or shame, but with an equal degree of relief, approved of Munich or accepted it.

A few months later and there was scarcely anyone, apart from the chief actors at the conference (and not even all of them), who could find any excuse for it.

So true it is that the natural way of putting an error right, when it has been committed by an entire nation, will always be a collective loss of memory.

Arnold J. Toynbee

CHAMBERLAIN AND HITLER—BRITAIN AND FRANCE

A Study of History in ten volumes and the controversy which has arisen over it have made Toynbee's name a household word in the Western world. Long before he published the first volume of his *Study* he had become familiar to students of international relations through his *Survey of International Affairs,* published under the auspices of the Royal Institute of International Affairs, and covering the years beginning with 1920 in one or more annual volumes. After World War II, during which the *Survey* was interrupted, others took up the main burden of compiling each year's record. For the second volume of the 1938 *Survey,* however, Toynbee wrote the introduction, from which the selection below is taken. His approach to Munich lies between the laudatory interpretation of Chamberlain's policy and the attribution of conspiratorial designs. Indeed, like most of the writers about Munich, he hardly mentions the Soviet Union. Does his explanation of Chamberlain's attitude and objectives make more or less sense than Macleod's, on the one hand, and Rothstein's, below, on the other? Does he agree or disagree with Noguères in his interpretation of French policy?

CHAMBERLAIN AND HITLER

CHAMBERLAIN and his colleagues were most anxious to do business[1] with the Germans, and they did not see why this should prove impossible simply because an undemocratic régime had been established in Germany. They recognized that it was now urgent to arrive at a satisfactory and desirable political understanding between Germany and the United Kingdom because they knew that for the last few years Germany had been rearming on an increasing scale and at an accelerating pace. It might per-

[1] Chamberlain's approach to the problem of dealing with Hitler cannot be understood unless it is recognized, appreciated, and kept constantly in mind that this British Prime Minister had spent the best part of his working life, not in politics, but in doing business in the commercial sense, and that he took it for granted that methods which, in his personal business experience, had proved fruitful for dealing with other business men would serve him equally well in the international arena in a gladiatorial encounter there with Hitler.

haps have been possible for Britain and France to veto this German rearmament in its earlier stages; but the opportunity of taking a firm line without the risk of becoming involved in war had been allowed to pass once for all when it was decided not to take action to eject the Reichswehr from the Rhineland after the reoccupation of the demilitarized zone on 7 March 1936. The British Government's attitude to this German *fait accompli* in 1936 had reflected an undoubtedly widespread feeling in Great Britain that it was only natural for the Germans to take advantage of an opportunity for liberating their country from one of the remaining discriminations to Germany's disadvantage in the international order as this had emerged from the First World War and the subsequent peace settlement. Two years later, similar considerations seem to have influenced the Chamberlain Government's view of Germany's still continuing rearmament and to have strengthened their unwillingness to

From Arnold J. Toynbee, "The Crisis over Czechoslovakia, January to September 1938," *Survey of International Affairs,* 1938, vol. 2, published by the Oxford University Press for the Royal Institute of International Affairs, pp. 4–9, 12–14, 20–21, 26–33.

adopt the vigorous counter-measures that were being urged upon them by people who were not carrying their heavy load of public responsibility.

After all, it could be argued, there was truth in Hitler's contention that so long as Germany had remained disarmed she had never been able to obtain any serious hearing for her claim to a revision of particular provisions of the Paris peace settlement which Germans regarded as inequitably onerous and which, as many non-Germans were ready to admit, could not be expected to remain unchanged in perpetuity, seeing that the country on which they had been imposed had not been deprived by her defeat in the last war of the man-power and the industrial resources that were the making of a Great Power. Hitler's method of exerting pressure by rearming was, admittedly, a dangerous game, and it had the further disadvantage of involving Germany and the other Western Powers in the expenditure on armaments of large sums of money which could otherwise have been put to productive uses. In Chamberlain's belief, however, it was still possible to call a halt to the armaments race by securing a fair settlement of reasonable German grievances; and he was ready to regard as reasonable not only the claim that the principle of national self-determination, which was rigorously applied in the Paris peace settlement in cases where it worked out to Germany's disadvantage, should be applied in cases where it would operate in her favour, but also the claim that Germany had the moral right to be reintrusted with the administration of some at least of her own former colonies or their equivalent. . . .

In general, Chamberlain probably agreed with Hitler's frequently expounded thesis that the stances in which the British Commonwealth and Germany had been placed by the gradual working out of their respective histories made it practicable for those two Powers to turn their faces resolutely in opposite directions without either of them needing to look back suspiciously over its shoulder at the other Power's proceedings in its own sphere. Even if he was not prepared to agree unreservedly with the argument

that the facts of physical and economic geography had endowed Germany with a natural sphere of interest in Central and Eastern Europe, Chamberlain did apparently regard it as an axiom that Britain had no interests in that region. In his view, if the British Government were to find themselves drawn, against their wishes, into participation in Central and East European politics, their role could only be that of an "honest broker," and their policy would be governed by two considerations: on the one hand, they would be prepared to show sympathy with German claims to benefit by some principle which had already been applied for the benefit of non-German peoples in this area; but, on the other hand, they would not be prepared to countenance Germany's pursuing any claims, however reasonable in themselves, by methods contrary to international order and inimical to the preservation of peace—e.g. by *coups de force* aiming at the production of irreversible *faits accomplis*, whether these illegitimate moves went the length of positive violence and bloodshed or achieved their aims by the mere threat of force.

Subject to the proviso—to which Chamberlain attached paramount importance—that Germany's demands must be presented in a reasonable manner for consideration according to an orderly procedure, the British Government seem to have looked forward without undue apprehension at the beginning of the year 1938 to the prospect of a readjustment in Germany's favour of the Paris peace settlement in Central Europe. At the same time, they could not fail to recognize that the satisfaction of Germany's claims would be a delicate business. The question of Austria's relation to a National Socialist Germany would be difficult enough to solve, though Austria was a nationally homogeneous German country. But the most formidable difficulties would not be encountered till it came to the question of the future of a German minority in Czechoslovakia which, in the frontier districts adjoining Silesia, Saxony, and Bavaria, was contiguous to the German Reich. As for the question arising over the so-called "Polish Corridor," this might have been expected to be more explosive than any issue between Germany and Czechoslovakia if Hitler himself had not rather surprisingly taken the initiative in 1934 in bringing about a *détente* in German-Polish relations which happily seemed to be standing the test of time. Though, in the process of readjustment, there were bound to be some awkward moments, the British Government felt that these could be faced with equanimity if there was a real prospect—as they believed there was—of arriving at a permanent settlement of Germany's claims which would allow Europe and the British Commonwealth to breathe more freely than had been possible at any time since the gathering of the storm that had broken over Europe in 1914.

The sincerity with which Chamberlain and a majority of his colleagues held these beliefs about the possibility of arriving at, not, perhaps, a gentleman's, but rather a business man's, agreement with Germany was demonstrated in January 1938, within the Cabinet's own sound-proof walls, by their willingness to sacrifice on the altar of appeasement no less precious a victim than their colleague Eden who had been Foreign Secretary since December 1935.

Eden's resignation—though this was not generally known until many years later—was the sequel to the rejection by the British Prime Minister of an offer, made by President Roosevelt on 12 January 1938, to invite the representatives of the British, French, German, and Italian Governments to meet in Washington for a discussion of the international situation. This decisive rebuff to an historic overture from Washington could only be interpreted as "midwinter madness" unless there was an unimpeachable warrant for the implied presupposition that Chamberlain had it in his power, by his own unaided diplomacy, to reach a lasting settlement with Hitler of all Hitler's claims without either departing from the procedure or going beyond the limits that Chamberlain himself had in mind. . . . Yet, when Chamberlain took his fatal action, there was at any rate no positive evidence whatsoever to lend colour to

Chamberlain's startlingly unconvincing, and in truth utterly mistaken, belief in the innocence of Hitler's intentions in the face of the abundant indications . . . that Hitler's character was demonic and his purpose sinister.

Moreover, even if there had been no presumptive evidence, in the concrete shape of previous acts and public pronouncements, that Hitler meant mischief and was not to be trusted, it will not have failed to strike the reader that— if the foregoing attempt at an *exposé* of Chamberlain's and his colleagues' state of mind and point of view is approximately correct—this Ministry was throwing over one of the governing principles of British foreign policy from which Chamberlain's predecessors in office had never departed, even when they were dealing with continental rulers whose record was less dubious (to use the language of *meiosis*) than Hitler's was. While one maxim of English foreign policy since the fortunate loss of Calais in 1558 had been generally to eschew the reacquisition of continental European possessions by England herself, another maxim to which the navigators of the British ship of state in international waters had been no less tenaciously faithful since 1688 was that a continental Power, however well-intentioned its rulers might profess, or even appear, to be, must not be permitted in any circumstances or on any consideration to expand its territorial possessions or political influence or military strength in Europe to a degree that would upset the Balance of Power by enduing this one Power with a preponderance over all possible combinations into which its neighbours, the United Kingdom included, might be able to enter for their common defence.

If we take this classical principle of traditional policy as our touchstone for testing the quality of Chamberlain's personal "new order" in the domain of foreign affairs, we shall see that Chamberlain was here taking a risk which was as unprecedented as it was immense. The measure of the innovation was given by the contrast between Chamberlain's policy towards Germany during the two and a half years preceding the outbreak of war with Germany in 1939 and the corresponding policy of previous British Governments during the ten years preceding the outbreak of war with Germany in 1914. While the Conservative and the succeeding Liberal Ministry in that decade had not been less eager for the preservation of peace than Chamberlain was in his day, they had not neglected to reply to ominous moves on the part of the Second German Reich by laying in advance the foundations of an *entente* whose combined strength might be expected to be a match for Germany and her allies if it were to come to war; and, on the classical theory of modern Western international politics, this countermeasure would (as in 1914–18 it did) at least produce the beneficial result of saving the world from subjugation if a war with Germany should unhappily break out, even if the taking of such precautions were to fail to have the very much more beneficial effect of deterring Germany from embarking on an actual attempt to achieve her aggressive ambitions. In the considerations determining Chamberlain's policy towards Germany on the eve of a second world war, if these considerations have been correctly analysed above, the effects that the contemplated concessions to Germany were bound in any circumstances to have upon the Balance of Power in Europe and overseas were either most deliberately ignored or most negligently overlooked.

*   *   *

While Hitler did not expect either France, Britain, or Russia to go to war with Germany for the sake of a pawn [Czechoslovakia] which Germany might be held to have it in her power already to take off the board, he did expect them to think of all his demands and his manoeuvres in terms of power politics, and therefore to go to war with him sooner or later, if they still had it in their power to take this step, in order to prevent him, if they could, from attaining a position of predominance in which he would have them at his mercy. Crediting the West

European Powers, as he did, with these warlike ultimate intentions, Hitler was already on the watch for opportunities, on his side, of forestalling their imaginary designs by spiking their guns or dealing them some crushing blow without giving them the time to take the initiative themselves.

In these guesses about current British foreign policy, Hitler was, of course, doubly in error. On the one hand, Chamberlain had not "written off the Czechs," and when Hitler eventually acted on this mistaken supposition of his by "clearing up this question" in his own fashion "in due course" on 15 March 1939, this action had the effect of opening Chamberlain's eyes at last to the truth that Hitler's real objective was not the limited and specious one of securing self-determination for Germans outside the Reich, but the unlimited and insufferable objective of winning for the German Reich itself a predominant position in the world by means of first acquiring a predominance in Central and Eastern Europe. When Chamberlain at last saw the truth, thanks to Hitler's revealing act of stripping the mask off his own face with his own hands, Chamberlain within the next three days reverted to a policy of upholding a threatened Balance of Power—by force of arms if it should have to come to that—which had been the standing policy of all previous British Governments since 1688 whenever a Power aiming at predominance had been on the war-path in the international wilderness. On the other hand, down to that moment —and this was the other point on which Hitler was in error on 5 November 1937 —Chamberlain was not thinking of Anglo-German relations in terms of the Balance of Power at all, and—incredible though this would have been to Hitler— he was not even thinking of Germany's expansion of her power in Central Europe in terms of "British interests" in the traditional meaning of the term. Even on 27 September 1938, twelve days after his first flight in an aeroplane had given him the means of appreciating, from recent personal experience, the appalling degree of proximity of all European countries to one another in the Air Age, Chamberlain once more proclaimed his own abiding blindness to the truth that Britain's destiny was now bound up with Czechoslovakia's in the transparent sincerity of his strangely naïve plaint in a broadcast to his fellow countrymen. "How horrible, fantastic, incredible it is that we should be digging trenches and trying on gas masks here because of a quarrel in a far-away country between people of whom we know nothing."

This thesis that Bohemia was situated on a different planet from England's Mother Earth had already been disputable in the seventeenth century when it had been a controversial issue in England on the eve and the morrow of the outbreak of the Thirty Years War; but King James I's timidity in 1618–19 was at least more excusable than Chamberlain's myopia in 1938. The tenacity with which this twentieth-century British Prime Minister clung to his startlingly anachronistic notions of contemporary European strategico-political geography was indicated when the misconception that he had revealed in his broadcast on 27 September reappeared in his speech in the House of Commons at Westminster on 28 September. "However remote this territory may be," the Prime Minister remarked in the course of this account of his stewardship, the British Government had been aware that a Czecho-German dispute, left to itself, "might give rise to a general conflagration."

If Chamberlain's words on 27 and 28 September 1938 had opened Hitler's eyes to Chamberlain's innocence, as Hitler's action on 15 March 1939 did open Chamberlain's to Hitler's guilt, we may guess that Hitler's emotional reaction would have been a lightning-swift succession of incredulity, contempt, and exultation. Even as it was, a Hitler who had never divined that Chamberlain was not concerned about the Balance of Power, must nevertheless have felt confident—at the latest, since the date of Eden's resignation—that the British Prime Minister and his colleagues were going to deliver themselves ineptly into the Austrian Man of Destiny's hands by letting slip the latest moment at which it would be possible for them to turn and fight with any pros-

pect of success. Hitler's blindness to the truth about Chamberlain remained as dense down to 15 March 1939 [destruction of the Czechoslovak state] as Chamberlain's blindness to the truth about Hitler remained down to the 18th of the same month; but, unlike Chamberlain's blindness, Hitler's eventually brought utter disaster on the purblind statesman's country. It was Hitler's Germany, not Chamberlain's Britain, that was to bite the dust in 1945.

* * *

Thus the incompatibility of the two different worlds in which the Germans and the British were at this time living side by side at point-blank bombing-range of one another drove the German and British Governments into working at cross purposes. On the British side, Chamberlain and his colleagues were seeking bona fide to open the way for Germany to achieve a limited territorial expansion in Central Europe within the limits allowed by an application of the principle of national self-determination and on condition that Germany did not resort to illegitimate means in pursuing legitimate objectives. On these terms, the British Government were prepared to acquiesce in the Reich's gaining additional territory, population, and resources without their allowing themselves to be influenced by any consideration of the effect of such an aggrandizement of Germany upon their own country's security. Meanwhile, on the German side, Hitler and his fellow conspirators had no intention of confining their ambitions within the bounds of an equitable revision of the political map on a fair interpretation of the principle of self-determination for Germans and non-Germans on a footing of equality; and they took it for granted that British Ministers were alive to the true scope of German aims and that they were set upon resisting the achievement of these German objectives by force of arms whenever, from the British standpoint, the time should seem ripe for going to war. The issue, as the Nazis saw it, on which the British had made up their minds to fight was not the vindication of international justice expressed in terms of national self-determination for all nations alike, and *a fortiori* was not the observance of the outward forms of decency, and the avoidance of flagrant acts of brutality, in the accomplishment of the process of "peaceful change" within equitable limits. If the British went to war, they would be fighting, so the Nazis believed, for the purpose of preserving the Balance of Power against changes in it to Germany's advantage which would incline it decidedly to the disadvantage of Great Britain. The belief, held by Hitler and Ribbentrop, that war between Germany and Great Britain was inevitable, was founded on the wildly erroneous idea that the mainspring of British policy *vis-à-vis* Germany was a calculation on the plane of power politics which British Ministers themselves were dismissing as *le cadet de leurs soucis* [the last thing they were troubling about] at this very time—and this with an impatience that was a certificate of their sincerity—when this traditional consideration was being rather shamefacedly pressed upon their attention by an impotent minority of their own fellow countrymen.

In these strange circumstances the British Government's steady insistence on their stipulation that even a legitimate German objective must not be pursued by illegitimate means was manifestly a factor of decisive importance in the working out of the international tragedy. To German minds this British stipulation must have seemed ineptly pedantic in so far as it could not be diagnosed as being grossly hypocritical; and British Ministers themselves, if cross-examined on their motives for attaching such importance to a proviso which might all too easily dwindle into a mere point of form, might have found it difficult to offer a rational explanation.

* * *

BRITAIN AND FRANCE

The change that came over Anglo-French relations before the recrudescence of war with Germany in 1939 was that the initiative in the shaping of French and British policy towards the rest of Europe, and particularly towards a resurgent Germany, was transferred to reluctant British hands from French hands that by this time were patently overwhelmed by the weight of a burden which British hands had previously declined to share. There had been premonitions of this transfer of the initiative during the Anglo-French consultations after Germany's military reoccupation of the demilitarized territory in the Rhineland on 7 March 1936. But this change in the relative positions of the two Powers did not become fully manifest till the arrival of the year 1938 brought the world under the anticipatory shadows of the Austrian and Czechoslovak crises.

What induced the British Ministers of the day, at a time when the clouds were once more manifestly gathering over the face of Europe, at last avowedly to take delivery of responsibilities which their predecessors had been so inauspiciously successful in nominally eluding so long as the skies had been more or less clear? The new feature in the international situation which goes farthest towards explaining this notable change in the British Government's attitude towards continental affairs is the unmistakable contemporaneous change in the attitude of France. By the beginning of the year 1938 it had become manifest that France had now ceased, whether for good or for evil, to carry on with the performance of her onerous fatigue-duty of standing sentinel over "the statute of Europe" inaugurated by the peace treaties of 1919–20. Her strategic capacity for resisting a fresh outbreak of German aggression had been paralysed by Germany's military reoccupation of the Rhineland on 7 March 1936, since this German move had deprived France of the possibility of replying to a German attack on Poland, Czechoslovakia, or Austria by striking at Germany's industrial heart in the Ruhr. At the same time, France's political capacity for standing up to Germany had been paralysed by a division of her house against itself, since, from 1936 onwards, a domestic class-war between the French industrial working-class and the French bourgeoisie had become so violent and so bitter as to eclipse, in many French hearts and minds, their perennial concern with the German peril at the very time when this peril was at last once again becoming serious. These were perhaps the two main causes of France's virtual abdication from her post-war hegemony of continental Europe; and one of the main consequences of France's retreat was to draw Great Britain forward.

The increasing readiness of France to leave the initiative in Europe to Great Britain, at a time when the danger of war was manifestly recurring, gave British Ministers both a motive for taking a more active hand in the game and a prospect of being able now, for the first time since the end of the First World War, to arrange for the game to be played, not on French, but on British lines. The motive that prompted Chamberlain and his colleagues was an eagerness to bring about a *détente* in the relations between a National Socialist Germany and her neighbours before Hitler should have time to precipitate a second world war by trying to take the law into his own hands. The prospect that attracted them was the illusory hope—examined in the first section of this introduction—that British diplomacy might be able, now that the post-war French policy of intransigently maintaining the existing "statute of Europe" was no longer standing in the way, to produce a durable settlement in Europe by arranging for the satisfaction of reasonable German demands by a respectable process of "peaceful change."

Though Chamberlain's policy of appeasement was doomed to failure from the start because it was based on a misreading of Hitler's character and intentions, it nevertheless had certain merits which become apparent when it is scrutinized against the foil of the policy—or impolicy—of contemporary Ministries in France. Ever since the making of the peace settlement after the First World War, the British had consistently held that a French policy of keeping the safety-valve closed *in saecula saeculorum* was bound, if persistently followed, to prove impracticable sooner or later; and now that France had at last abandoned her obstructive policy at a moment when the boiler was threatening to explode, it was surely the part of wisdom to unthrottle a safety-valve that was at last accessible to British hands, perilously late though the hour might now be for taking this obvious elementary precaution. A second merit of Chamberlain's policy which shone up brightly against a nebulous French background was its most un-French insistence on the necessity of cutting one's coat according to the cloth.

If it was true, as it was, that as a result of the West European Powers' decision not to attempt to reverse Germany's military reoccupation of the demilitarized zone in the Rhineland on 7 March 1936, it had ceased to be within the power of France, with or without British support, to give any effective aid to her East European allies in the event of their becoming the victims of German attacks, then it was obvious that the only remaining alternative to eventual German attacks, to which these derelict *saisonsstaaten* would be bound to succumb, was for these prospective Central and East European "Ethiopias" to agree with their German adversary quickly while they were in the way with him. If there were any sincerity at all in Hitler's professions, there was perhaps a chance that these threatened states on the far side of the Reich might be able to purchase their lives at the sacrifice of some of their limbs. If the sacrifices demanded of them were genuinely to be confined to those cessions of territory that would meet Hitler's claim that a principle of national self-determination which had already been applied to Germany's disadvantage should now also be applied in Germany's favour, then the price of survival, however painful, would be neither inequitable nor unlimited. It was also manifest that these menaced Central and East European states were likely to obtain better terms if, instead of being left face to face with a militarily irresistible Germany, to make the best terms that they could in such untoward circumstances, they could benefit by the good offices of a Britain and a France whose united voices might even now be expected to carry some weight with Hitler—especially if he could be convinced that the two West European Powers were intervening in the encounter between the wolf and the lamb, not as advocates retained in advance to work exclusively for the lamb's defence, but as honest and open-minded brokers who were determined to give even a wolf his due. On these diplomatic lines there might still be hope of the West European Powers' being able to perform an appreciable political service for Germany's Central and East European neighbours. And what service of a military order could they hope to perform for them in present circumstances? French Ministers had no answer to give when, on 12 March 1938, Halifax asked them how they were in fact proposing to give Czechoslovakia military assistance in the event of Germany's attacking her.

British policy also parted company with French policy in being governed by a sober unwillingness to incur political obligations that the country would not have the strength to honour by military action in the last extremity. This consideration weighed heavily in both Halifax's and Chamberlain's calculations. On the morrow of the First World War, Great Britain's proportionate reduction of her land armaments had been more drastic than France's, and, for the sake of economy, she had abandoned her post-war lead in the development of the mechanized warfare which she had inaugurated by the invention of the tank, after having carried her pioneer work far enough for it to prove invaluable to a never successfully liquidated German General Staff. Thereafter, when Germany started to rearm in earnest after Hitler's advent to power, Great Britain and France alike were caught napping. Within the period from 1933 to 1938, they allowed Germany, starting from zero, to win a preponderance over their own combined strength in the air. This negligence on the part of both Governments was inexplicable and unpardonable; but Great Britain did at least begin to rearm, however inadequately, from 1935 onwards, and Chamberlain, when he became Prime Minister in 1937, carried on this rearmament, with an eye to providing himself with a minimum fund of military power for underwriting a policy of maximum political conciliation. France, on the other hand, persisted, until after the international crisis of 1938 had descended upon her, in maintaining a verbally uncompromising front while allowing herself, under the handicap of the forty-hours' week, to fall farther and farther behind Germany in an armaments race in which Hitler had long since set the pace. Chamberlain's pressing inquiry into the state of French armaments during the Anglo-French talks in London on 25 September 1938 was as disconcerting to his French colleagues as their inability to give him any satisfactory answers to his pertinent questions was disturbing to Chamberlain on his side.

The contrast between Britain's tardy and partial yet appreciable rearmament and France's virtual abandonment of the effort to keep abreast of Germany in military preparations, as well as in ultimate war-potential, became all the more striking when it was recalled that France was bound by treaties to give military assistance to Czechoslovakia, Poland, Rumania, Jugoslavia, and the Soviet Union in the event of a *casus foederis* arising, whereas Great Britain had no such treaty-commitment to any continental European Power. At a meeting of the League Council at Geneva in May 1938, before the onset of the abortive crisis over Czechoslovakia on the 21st of that month, Bonnet begged Halifax to save France from having to make the choice between defaulting on her commitments to Czechoslovakia and going to war with Germany by putting British pressure on the Czechoslovak Government to whatever degree might be necessary in order to force them to give satisfaction to the Sudetendeutsch. When the storm eventually broke in the autumn of 1938, a formally committed French Government again besought a formally uncommitted British Government on 13 September of that year to move heaven and earth to save France from being confronted with a *casus foederis* arising out of the Franco-Czechoslovak Treaty; and French Ministers who had suggested that a way out might be found in the convening of an international conference did not quarrel with Chamberlain's decision to try the alternative course of proposing a personal meeting between himself and Hitler. They did, though, meanly seek, after the event, to cast on British shoulders the odium for the success of Chamberlain's *tour de force* of momentarily preserving a peace which the French Government and people had been even more desperately eager to preserve than their British partners were. When British and French Ministers conferred on 18 September, as the Munich crisis was approaching its climax, they found themselves in agreement in being bent, alike, on "peace at almost any price"; and they consequently agreed in bowing to the terms that Hitler had dictated to Chamberlain at Berchtesgaden on 15 September. Yet, in breaking the news to the French public, a French official spokesman declared that the French Government had been forced to accept the British Government's proposals for capitulating to Hitler because British Ministers had refused to commit themselves to giving France British military support except in the event of the integrity of France herself being threatened. While it is true that British Ministers had continued to take this deplorable line, the evidence also makes it clear that this was not the determining factor in inducing French Ministers to fall in with British policy. The aid that French Ministers were most eager to obtain from British Ministers at this critical moment was not military but diplomatic. They wanted the British Government to save the French Government from having to honor their treaty obligations to Czechoslovakia by going to war with Germany; and they would have been every whit as anxious to elude war with Germany, even if they had had explicit assurances in advance from the British Government that Britain would come to France's military assistance in a French war with Germany in which France had engaged for the defence of Czechoslovakia and not of France herself against a German attack.

Yet neither the French Government's anxiety to wriggle out of their military obligations to Czechoslovakia nor their concomitant anxiety to evade the odium of their unheroic attitude by misrepresenting their own motives to their British colleagues' detriment can excuse British Ministers for having provided the French Government with such a pretext, however unsubstantial and insincere the French apologia might be. The truth was that, while an ingrained French habit of using words as if these were effective substitutes for facts and deeds was as disquieting as it was exasperating to French Ministers' British colleagues, British Ministers, on their side, continued to carry on the inter-war British activity of breaking French hearts for the sake of preserving the fatuous luxury of uttering words as empty as any that issued from French lips.

On 12 and 24 March 1938, British Ministers were still saying to French Ministers that it was contrary to British policy to enter into commitments over hypothetical future contingencies, and that the British Government were unwilling to advise France as to what her policy towards Czechoslovakia ought to be. As late as 22 May they warned the French Government not to reckon on Britain's at once taking joint military action with France to preserve Czechoslovakia against German aggression if France were to go to war with Germany on that account; and, incredible though this would be if there were not chapter and verse of documentary evidence to attest its truth, the same disheartening British official forms of words were churned out twice again in the apocalyptic month of September 1938....

Even when British Ministers and British publicists were airing their views of the form and extent of British aid to France in the event of another war in which the British would be fighting side by side with the French against the Germans, they seemed sometimes to go out of their way to discourage their past and future French allies.

British spokesmen seemed, for example, positively to take a delight in pointing out that, in another war with a German Reich which had grown militarily still more formidable than ever before in the act of passing out of the Hohenzollern second embodiment into its Hitlerian third avatar, there could be no question of Great Britain's being able, even at a greatly reduced speed, to place at the French army's side, on continental European *terra firma,* a British expeditionary force at all comparable in relative strength to the magnificently trained and equipped force that, in 1914, she had brought into action so swiftly and with such far-reaching effects on the outcome of the all-important first phase of the First World War....

Conversely, the French behaved almost as if they were deliberately depreciating to zero the valuation of their efficacy as allies in the esteem of British neighbours whose aid they were so eager to be able to count upon in the ever more probable event of war with Germany breaking out again. The French working class gave anxious British observers the impression that they had forgotten the German peril in their determination to preserve and defend the tardy concessions—above all, the forty-hours' week—which they had recently wrung out of reluctant French employers, while the French middle class gave the impression that a French working class which they were apt to identify with a band of French Communist agitators, and French Communists whom they were equally apt to identify with their Russian principals, had taken Germany's place as "Enemy Number One" in bourgeois French eyes. The apparently incurable instability of French Ministries, even in the face of the gravest international crises, was another weakness of France which—just because it was coeval with the Third Republic (to leave out of account the more violent and hardly less kaleidoscopic vicissitudes of French political régimes during the eighty-two years 1789–1871)—was as disturbing as it was exasperating to British statesmen on the eve of a second world war. Not the least disquieting feature of contemporary French political life from a British standpoint was that some of the personalities that showed the greatest ability to maintain a continuous footing on the moving staircase of a French political flux were politicians whose characters and records were not such as to inspire confidence in the minds either of their own countrymen or of their British partners.

When Hitler ran over, as he did from time to time, this array of perennial causes of misunderstanding and mistrust between the governments and peoples of the two West European Powers, he must have felt that the stars in their courses were fighting against these Canaanites that his German Israel was girding itself to smite and overwhelm.

Andrew Rothstein

THE MUNICH CONSPIRACY

At the time of Munich and ever since, some writers have insisted that the true explanation of the Agreement lay in the plan or plot or conspiracy of the British and French governments to turn Hitler against Soviet Russia. No one has more fully documented this view than Andrew Rothstein, who was a Tass correspondent at the time of Munich and has since published such studies as a *History of the U.S.S.R.* (London, 1950) and *Peaceful Coexistence* (London, 1955). Although the selections here reprinted are a small part of his full-length book, they indicate his methods of interpretation and the gist of his conclusions. Does he read into the primary sources, especially into the "dots and omissions," more than is justified? Note that his assumptions about Chamberlain's motivation are quite different from those of Macleod or of Toynbee. Are they more or less plausible?

From Andrew Rothstein, *The Munich Conspiracy* (London: Lawrence & Wishart, 1958), pp. 108–110, 114, 116–117, 255–257, 259–261, 263–271. © Lawrence & Wishart, Ltd., 1958. Reprinted by permission of the publisher.

[A BRIEF CALENDAR]

FROM that time onwards [signature of the Munich Agreement], as was remarked at the League Assembly on the evening of the 30th by one of the bitter wits always to hand on such occasions, the uppermost thought in the minds of other States was that "you may at any time become someone's Czechoslovakia" —and that in their dealings with Great Britain in particular, they must above all avoid becoming a victim of the British Government's transactions in the name of peace.

But a particularly important aspect of this was the fact that, except for one occasion on September 23, at Geneva (of which more later), the British Government kept the Soviet Union at arm's length during the whole period from March to the end of September. So much was clear to the public, and it was commented on more than once in the House of Commons. But the publication of the diplomatic papers since the war, and particularly those of the British Foreign Office, has underlined that the interest of the British Government and its officials throughout was to avoid contact with the Soviet Government as much as possible, to reject its suggestions where offered, and to spread as much distrust of and hostility to the idea of co-operating with the U.S.S.R. as it could. A brief calendar will suffice:

MARCH 23. Halifax tells French Ambassador that the Soviet Note of March 17 had no "great value."

He tells Maisky that the British Government rejects the Soviet proposals (March 24) [to take "collective actions" to stop the "further development of aggression"].

APRIL 19. British Ambassador reports from Moscow that there is no reason "for doubting the possibility of a revolution if this country were to become involved in war." The economic system would not be likely "to stand up to the strain." There would be "a complete breakdown of all supplies and communications." Any defeats "could not fail to produce a collapse which might well overturn the régime."

The military attaché produces even more idiotic "information" (e.g. that "there might be a danger to the régime in mobilisation," and that he doubts "whether there are now available men who are capable of commanding armies in the event of war").

APRIL 29.   Lord Halifax duly reports in this sense at the conference with French Ministers, doubting if the U.S.S.R. "could make any contribution at all to the protection of Czechoslovakia."

MAY 15.   British Chargé d'Affaires in Moscow expatiates at length on the same lines as on April 19 (e.g. that the Soviet General Staff and High Command are in "appalling chaos and disorganisation"), with this gem: "the Russians are Asiatics, more so now than at any period since Peter the Great."

MAY 22.   He follows this up by forecasting that "the Soviet Union is unlikely to go to war in defence of Czechoslovakia."

MAY 27.   Halifax suggests that the Chargé d'Affaires should try and get Litvinov to exercise pressure on the Czechoslovak Communists: the Chargé d'Affaires prudently declines, saying it would be rejected.

MAY 31.   British military attaché in Moscow reports that the Soviet Government "will find any pretext to avoid the necessity of having to fulfil its engagements to Czechoslovakia and France."

JUNE 14.   British Minister in Warsaw reports that the Chief of the Polish Staff has informed the British military attaché (with a wealth of detail) that "Russia would very soon reach a crisis which would put her out of action not for months but for years."

JULY 16.   Bonnet tells British Ambassador Phipps—and Phipps agrees—that Beneš asking him to sound Russia about help, in the event of war with Germany, showed "what a dangerous frame of mind he is in."

SEPTEMBER 2.   Phipps reports that Bonnet has been "pestered lately by the Soviet Ambassador, acting on instructions from M. Litvinov, to show more firmness in Czechoslovakia and to urge greater firmness on the part of His Majesty's Government."

Bonnet asked what help the Soviets would give if the Germans attacked Czechoslovakia, "but so far there is no reply" (in fact it had been given that very day—the first time it was asked).

SEPTEMBER 6.   Bonnet tells Phipps that Litvinov's reply is that the U.S.S.R. will (i) wait until France begins to fulfil her obligations, (ii) then bring the matter before Geneva. Meanwhile he proposes a joint Anglo-Franco-Soviet declaration "that they will keep the peace, if necessary by force" (an impudent travesty, as will be seen later).

SEPTEMBER 8.   Halifax "notes" Litvinov's real proposals, reported on September 3 by Churchill, who thought them "of the first importance" [Gathering Storm (Boston, 1948), p. 296].

SEPTEMBER 10.   British Minister in Warsaw urges that France should make every effort in Moscow "to prevent the Soviet Union taking any measure which might determine Poland to throw herself into the German camp."

SEPTEMBER 11.   Bonnet rejects Litvinov's proposal of discussions at Geneva: British Government agrees.

SEPTEMBER 23.   Halifax instructs British delegation at Geneva to ask the Soviet delegation about what they would do if Czechoslovakia were at war with Germany (the first such enquiry). Litvinov tells them (elaborating on proposals he had made publicly, in the Assembly, on September 21). Nothing more ever heard. Churchill calls it "indeed astonishing" that "the Soviet offer was in effect ignored" (op. cit., p. 305).

SEPTEMBER 29.   Halifax calls in Maisky to tell him that the U.S.S.R. was not invited to Munich because Hitler and Mussolini would refuse to sit down with its representatives.

That is all—a proud record of diplomacy: sixteen occasions in seven months of 1938 (nearly half of them in September) on which the Soviet Union's attitude was discussed by British diplomats, in a form thought suitable for publication by the editors of Documents on British Foreign Policy! Most of the sixteen occasions were for the purpose of recording or spreading imbecile and malicious tittle-tattle. On only three of the sixteen occasions was there direct discussion with representatives of the Soviet Government—two of them formally to reject Soviet offers of co-operation, the third (despite promises to keep in touch) amounting to the same thing. Not once was it thought worth while to invite a leading member of the Soviet Government to London, or to send a member of the Inner Cabinet to Moscow —if only to clear up alleged doubts as to where the Soviet Government stood.

This was quite an important aspect of the Chamberlain Government's diplomacy during the months from March to September, 1938; although an assessment of its meaning must be reserved for a later chapter.

* * *

AN INCONVENIENT PACT

What neither the general public nor, possibly, the Czechoslovak Government knew was the background to 1938 so far as the Franco-Soviet pact of mutual assistance was concerned. It was Czechoslovakia which was the immediate beneficiary of that pact, since Germany was less likely to attack either of its signatories than her southern neighbour, if she had the free choice. The fact that the signature of the pact was followed immediately by one between the U.S.S.R. and Czechoslovakia (May 2, 1935, and May 16, 1935) was a simple recognition of this fact. But after the Franco-Soviet pact was signed, successive French Governments refused to make the necessary preparations to implement it by arranging for staff agreements between the military authorities of the two countries—such as their predecessors, in 1892 and 1912, had concluded with the Tsarist Government of Russia, and as had been argeed when the pact was signed in Paris.

Post-war French memoirs of men who held high office leave no doubts. [According to these memoirs, on some half dozen occasions the French turned down Soviet efforts to negotiate a military agreement.]

* * *

These various occasions may or may not have been all known to the Czechoslovak authorities (though their military chiefs were in very close relations with the French General Staff). But the re-

sult at any rate was obvious—no military agreement between France and the U.S.S.R., hence nothing practical done to ensure that the treaty of 1935 would operate in case of German aggression. That being so, was it likely that the treaties with Czechoslovakia were intended to operate?

These, then, were the traditions established between 1935 and 1938 by the governments of MM. Laval, Flandin, Blum, Chautemps and Daladier. Therefore professional diplomats should not have been surprised. The peoples were another matter: they had no access to State papers, international negotiations or diplomatic gossip. For the majority of the common people the events of 1938 came with bewildering suddenness.

In the case of France the position today, when we come to examine those events more closely, is complicated by the fact that its Foreign Office archives nearly all perished during the war. It is said that they have been partly reconstituted with the help of the files kept in French Embassies abroad; in any case, there have been no such collections of documents published on French foreign policy as those on British or German. It is from the latter archives—to the extent that the British editors (and American, in the case of the captured German documents) have made it possible—that we have to draw our information on French diplomacy in 1938: coupled with press information at the time, and memoirs of varying value mostly (not all) published since 1945.

What picture emerges? Above all, one of complete co-operation with the British Government in imposing surrender of Czechoslovakia to Hitler—in spite of the programme of isolating and destroying France outlined in *Mein Kampf*.

* * *

WHY DID THEY DO IT?

Even if there were no documents to demonstrate the contrary, it cannot seriously be contended that what was obvious to British and French diplomats on the spot, to special correspondents and political journalists, to military men of experience and to their secret agents, was hidden from the Ministers governing Britain and France in 1938.

They knew very well, from diplomatic dispatches and other reports, that the whole "Sudeten German" agitation was a purposeful swindle engineered from Berlin, and that the mass of German-speaking citizens of Czechoslovakia, whatever grievances they had, had no desire to be forced under the bloody tyranny of Hitler's Reich instead of getting their grievances remedied in Czechoslovakia. The British and French Governments, whatever they told their respective publics, knew perfectly well that the Munich terms were no better than those of Godesberg, and their own precious "international guarantee" not worth the paper it was written on—except to tide them over a difficult moment in face of public opinion. They were well aware that they *had* excluded the U.S.S.R., and that—if they had put all the facts before their peoples—no one would have cried out that Czechoslovakia was "a far-away country," with a people "of whom we know nothing." *They* did not require generals to tell them that, even if Czechoslovakia were partly ravaged in the first onset of war, that would not decide its outcome: and that, however great their deficiencies in armaments, the real balance of strength in 1938, if they called in the U.S.S.R. soon enough, would be overwhelmingly on their side* before ever a question of war arose, and probably would prevent it. Nor were they so uninformed—for then they would have been almost alone in their respective countries—as to be ignorant of the step-by-step tactics of conquest pursued by Hitler, in applying the policy of *Mein Kampf*, or of the possibilities opened to him, both in Eastern and Western Europe, if Czechoslovakia were destroyed. That is to say, they were well aware that, in the literal sense, peace would be more, not less, threatened by Munich.

No one who takes the trouble to read

either the diplomatic documents or the memoirs of the time—or even some competent account of how the machinery of government works in Britain and France —could have the slightest illusion about the foregoing. Chamberlain, Daladier and their associates could only have been blind to these things if they wanted to be blind.

Therefore the real question is, *why* did they want to be blind? *In what sense* did they hope that peace was strengthened by Munich? Or let us put it in another way. The excuses and apologies they made after the event are not important: all these men were politicians, trained up and well versed in a system which puts a premium on promising one thing at elections and doing another after winning them. To look at what they said in public, while carrying out their operation on the flesh of the Czechoslovak people, would be as helpful as listening to the cheap-jack's patter in the market, instead of looking at the goods he is selling. But what did they really have in mind, in doing what they did between March and September, 1938?

In trying to answer this question, we should take into account one remarkable circumstance. On all sides, during these fatal months, responsible people were telling each other how dangerous it was for them to go to war, because the Soviet Union and Communism would be likely to win it.

On April 30, 1938, Bonnet told Welczeck, the German Ambassador in Paris, that in the event of world war "all Europe would perish, and both victor and vanquished would fall victims to world Communism." On May 10 the same opinion was conveyed to Welczeck by Paul Reynaud, Minister of Justice and Bonnet's colleague: war would be a catastrophe "from which Europe would never recover, with the possible exception of Russia, remote and already living under Communism." On May 22 it was Daladier's turn. War, he told Welczeck, "would mean the utter destruction of European civilisation. Into the battle zones, devastated and denuded of men, Cossack and Mongol hordes would pour, bringing to Europe a new 'culture.' This

---

* "It would not be correct to say that our military weakness was the principal cause of the Munich agreement," wrote one of its chief architects, Sir Samuel Hoare (Lord Templewood), in his memoirs, *Nine Troubled Years* (1945), p. 289.

must be prevented, even if it entailed great sacrifices." On the same day, in Berlin, Nevile Henderson [British ambassador] was conveying to Ribbentrop [German foreign minister] the same terrifying information: he couldn't guarantee that Great Britain would stand aside if Germany used forcible measures—and "only those will benefit from such a catastrophe who wish to see the destruction of European civilisation."

The idea was not entirely novel to the Germans: but on June 20, in a memorandum presented to Ribbentrop by Weizsäcker [state secretary in the foreign office], warning him against a policy which would bring Britain and France into war with Germany too soon, we read again that "the common loser with us would be the whole of Europe, the victors chiefly the non-European continents and the anti-social powers." However, the French Ambassador in Moscow joined in the lecturing some time in August. Expressing the hope that there would be no Franco-German conflict, "you know as well as I do for whom we are working if we come to blows," Coulondre told von der Schulenberg [German ambassador in Moscow]. The next day, in Prague, Beneš was telling the Henleinite leaders that "he was only afraid of two things, a war and, after it, a Bolshevik revolution." And the complete unity of Germany's actual and possible opponents on this point was again underlined for her rulers the next day again (August 25), when a cable from the German Legation in Prague informed them that the Secretary of the British Legation, in conversation with both journalists and diplomats, was declaring: "If it came to war between Germany, France and Britain, the only ones to benefit would be the Soviets." . . .

But if this was the universally agreed prospect, and if—as was obvious from the experience of the years 1933–8, and still more of the months from March to September, 1938—the ambitions of the Nazi leaders in a revived imperialist Germany were creating the threat of a new world war which must bring revolution in its train, why encourage them? Why not prevent war? Why not enlist

the support of the Soviet Union in putting it off? These questions were all the more reasonable because Stalin at no time and in no way was extolling the virtues of war. On the contrary. In the very same speech of January, 1934, which had become known throughout the world, Stalin had said that, without having "to sing the praises of the Versailles Treaty, we merely do not agree to the world being flung into the abyss of a new war on account of that treaty." He had, moreover, in referring to the restoration of normal relations between the U.S.S.R. and the U.S.A. (in December, 1933), emphasised that it improved the chances of preserving peace. And in 1938 itself the Soviet Government, as we have seen, had repeatedly offered to co-operate in preserving peace.

Why were the Soviet offers rejected, if the British and French were so afraid of the revolutionary consequences of a war? Why was the chance of calling a halt to the declared organisers of world conquest, and therefore of world war, thrown away? Why did the British and French Governments prefer yet a further settlement with Hitler at someone else's expense, after all the previous deals of 1933–8—and even though it meant gambling with their own security in Europe —to a full understanding with the U.S.S.R. which would have inflicted such a check on Hitler as must inexorably have broken his prestige among his own people?

The answer to these questions is the answer to the question at the head of this . . . [section].

To some extent it was given, of course, by the experience of the years prior to 1938. And behind the scenes much was said in those years to make that clear. Some examples were given in the first part of this book; here are more. In 1935 Chamberlain himself, then Chancellor of the Exchequer, had replied to A. V. Ozersky, the Soviet Trade Representative in London, enquiring about credit and other facilities for expanding trade between the two countries: "But why should we assist our worst enemy!" The Franco-Soviet pact of mutual assistance was never implemented by France in 1936 and 1937, wrote the French Ambassador in Moscow during those years, "because of the prejudices teeming in France against the Soviets and their régime." Geoffrey Dawson, the editor of *The Times* (writes his biographer), was, in October and November, 1937, when his friend Lord Halifax went to Berlin, "fully cognisant" that "Nazi Germany undoubtedly stood as a wedge between Russian Communism and the West," and that to ring Germany about "with vigilant allied States, sometimes masquerading as the League of Nations, like trained elephants round a tiger in the jungle to prevent her expansion in any direction beyond the limits imposed twenty years ago" was a process which should be stopped—otherwise it must "lead inevitably to war and to the downfall of civilisation in the West." That is to say, the "West" had more in common with Hitler than with the U.S.S.R.: if Hitler were overthrown on account of his "expansion," it would mean the overthrow of civilisation: if he expanded only against "Russian Communism," even at the expense of that "masquerade" known as the League of Nations, it would be a different story— and it was worth risking world war in the future for the sake of that. Then Chamberlain, Eden and Halifax met the French Premier Chautemps, his Foreign Minister Delbos and Léger, the permanent head of the Foreign Ministry, at the end of November, 1937 (just after Halifax's visit to Hitler). Chamberlain liked Chautemps. "He was quick and witty and, as it seemed to me, quite candid and straightforward. He did not conceal his dislike for Soviet Russia. . . ." These dots are in the extract quoted by Chamberlain's biographer: a pity they should come just at that point.

Here one should draw attention to the special role of "dots," and other signs of omission and ellipsis, in the documents of the time. Again and again—in memoirs, diaries, collections of diplomatic documents—they appear and reappear, with almost invariable regularity, whenever the dangerous subject of the Soviet Union arises. In the same way masses of documents suddenly disappear, just when they would throw a good deal of

light on what the spokesmen of "civilisation in the West" were saying about the Soviet Union. . . .

For these very reasons it should not be expected that, on the all-important question of the rejection of the Soviet offers, the published collections of official documents or memoirs of statesmen would contain memoranda or dispatches setting forth clearly the real reasons why the British and French Governments preferred agreement with Hitler—and the consequent aggression—to agreement with the Soviet Union. Dots and omissions are too convenient a device. One must fall back on circumstantial evidence in most cases. Only on a few occasions does a slip or chance oversight give a pointer: but when it does, the direction is always the same.

Thus on January 16, 1938, Chamberlain wrote to a friend in the U.S.A. that he was "about to enter upon a fresh attempt to reach a reasonable understanding with both Germany and Italy," and hoped for help in this from the U.S.A., particularly when it came to hinting to Hitler that overwhelming force might be used against him. In his diary, on February 19, he entered that from the first he had been "trying to improve relations with the two storm centres, Berlin and Rome." We know already, from his speech in the House of Commons on February 21 in which he developed this idea, that he excluded the Soviet Union as "half-Asiatic" from his four-Power scheme for settling the peace of Europe. These sentiments, "admirable as they sound out of their context, were alarming to devotees of collective security who lived on the eastern side of the Axis, remote from Britain and France, and who looked to the Soviet Republic to join at least with France, if not also with Britain in their defence. They were correspondingly encouraging to the declared enemies of the League of Nations at Berlin." How much more alarming to the one, and encouraging to the other, Chamberlain's sentiments would have sounded, a month later, if they had known that, in a letter to another correspondent, he had written of "the Russians stealthily and cunningly pulling all the strings behind the scenes to get us involved in war with Germany"—because, three days before, they had offered their co-operation in stopping further aggression (Litvinov's proposal of March 17), at a time when Germany was "flushed with triumph" and Britain was unable to "beat her to her knees in a reasonable time"!

Would not both have concluded that, should Hitler, flushed with triumph, have decided to attack the U.S.S.R., with or without the agreement of Poland, and whether or not he stopped by the way to devour Czechoslovakia, Chamberlain would have heaved a sigh of relief . . .? The information was not disclosed at the time: but it provides a key to Munich. It was, indeed, shortly after this (April 4, 1938) that U.S. Ambassador Davies wrote from Moscow to Stephen Early, President Roosevelt's secretary: "Russia might be a helpful bulwark for the protection of international peace. The European democracies, however, seem deliberately to play into the hands of the Fascists in the effort to isolate completely the great power that is here from the rest of the world, and particularly from France and England. It is a pity, but it is true."

What the minds of "the European democracies" were running on was in fact not very difficult to understand, for people who read the newspapers carefully, even then. But they would have been helped had they known that, on April 25, the British War Minister (Leslie Hore-Belisha) had a talk with the chief of the French General Staff about Germany's policy after the annexation of Austria —and "saw her ambitions, at least at first, towards Eastern Europe." This remark indicates the real background to Chamberlain's complacent statement— at the meeting of British and French Ministers in London, three days later— that "he wondered if the picture of the European situation was as black as Daladier had painted it." Churchill himself, only a few days before, had expressed privately the fear that Chamberlain intended to follow up the Italo-British Agreement signed on the 16th (giving Italy virtually a free hand in Ethiopia

and Spain while the League of Nations was still pledged to support both) with "something even more specious with Germany, which will lull the British public while letting the German armed strength grow and German designs in the East of Europe develop."

Churchill himself, however, did not always take pains to discourage those designs, judging by the translated record in the German archives of a conversation on July 14, 1938, between himself and Foerster, head of the Danzig Nazis, who was on a visit to England. At one point, the record runs: "I remarked that I did not believe that Germany really feared Russia, to which he replied that they knew for a fact of the existence of Russian airfields in Czechoslovakia, from which an attack could be launched on Berlin in half an hour. I replied that, in my opinion, it would be quite possible, as part of a general European agreement, to pledge Britain and France to come to Germany's assistance with all their forces should she be the victim of an unprovoked attack on the part of Russia through Czechoslovakia, or in any other way. He asked who was to determine who was the aggressor? I replied that the aggressor would be the nation that first forcibly crossed the frontier of another nation."

But would the agreement work the other way, so far as the U.S.S.R. was concerned? On that Churchill seems to have said nothing. Naturally, this may be represented as a manoeuvre, only intended to draw Foerster out by dangling before him the bait of a one-sided guarantee (such as was implicit in Chamberlain's plans and speeches of February and March). But the curious thing is that it fitted in very well with a suggestion made by Chamberlain himself, during his talks with Hitler at Berchtesgaden on September 15. "The British Prime Minister asked whether German objections regarding this role of Czechoslovakia" (which Hitler had described as "a menace to Germany—a spearhead in Germany's side") "would cease to exist if it were possible so to alter the relations between that country and Russia that, on the one hand, Czechoslovakia would be released from her obligations to Russia *in the case of an attack on that country* and, on the other hand, if she like Belgium no longer had the possibility of obtaining assistance from Russia or another country" (the record kept by Schmidt, Hitler's interpreter; Chamberlain's own minute, made later for the Cabinet, spoke of Czechoslovakia not providing facilities for Soviet planes on her airfields).

Thus in both cases, in July and September, the idea put to the Germans was that, if Hitler could find some way of attacking the U.S.S.R. which did not draw Britain into war, by the necessity of assisting France, the way might be open to him, if he wanted it.

*   *   *

So much for the diplomatic documents before September, 1938. They begin to suggest the true explanation of British and French policy at Munich—that it was an agreement to let Hitler take Czechoslovakia, in the hope that it was but a temporary stopping place on the road to a German war with the Soviet Union. The reader will remember that this was precisely the explanation which Mr. Gedye got in official, diplomatic and political quarters in London, long before Munich. When we come to the memoirs of other eye-witnesses of that time, of participants in the tragedy, men who cannot be accused of Communist sympathies, we hear it again and again.

Beneš wrote: "Munich with all its catastrophic European consequences would not have occurred but for the hostility of Western Europe towards the Soviet Union and the differences between them. . . . The exclusion of the Soviet Union from all pre- and post-Munich discussions was equivalent—in the Soviet view —to an attack against the Soviet Union and to an attempt to secure its complete isolation. Moscow *rightly*" (the italics are Beneš') "feared that this fatal step could soon lead to a military attack by Germany against the Soviet Union." If Moscow was right in *fearing*, Chamberlain could hardly avoid *hoping*: that is the logic of Beneš' words.

Wheeler-Bennett, present in Czechoslovakia in September, in fact writes: "This willingness to see Hitler dominant in Central and Eastern Europe was not, however, merely a by-product of the general trend of British diplomacy. It was of far greater significance than that, and represented one of the prime factors in the whole political situation. Behind the general desire for peace and for an 'accommodation' with Hitler then lay, if not in the mind of Mr. Chamberlain himself at any rate in the minds of some of his advisers, the secret hope that, if German expansion could be directed towards the East, it would in time come into collision with the rival totalitarian imperialism of Soviet Russia. In the conflict which would ensue both the forces of National Socialism and Communism would be exhausted. . . . It was believed by those who held these opinions that Bolshevik Russia was of greater danger to Britain than Nazi Germany."

Paul-Boncour, dismissed by Daladier in April, 1938, because he favoured a policy of close political and military co-operation with the U.S.S.R., wrote in his memoirs (in 1942, after the defeat of France) that it was "the fear of Communism" (in this case the U.S.S.R.) "which made the frogs ask for the Führer who would protect them. This helped them to get the Anschluss, Munich, the suppression of Czechoslovakia. This had interfered with the utilisation of the Franco-Soviet pact, to the point of ruining it." This was the sentiment, he said, which had "hung so heavily on French foreign policy since 1936."

Coulondre wrote from his Embassy in Moscow to Bonnet, on October 4, 1938 (a document not included in the French Yellow Book): "The Munich agreement, so pregnant with consequences for the future of all Europe, of which many of the values will doubtless have to be revised, is particularly heavy with menace for the Soviet Union." Is it to be supposed that Chamberlain did not see what Coulondre did? He continued: "With the neutralisation of Czechoslovakia, the road to the South-East is henceforth open to Germany. Will there be any Powers willing and able to prevent her entering it, or halting on it before she reaches Russia, in order to see there the *Lebensraum* announced in *Mein Kampf*? This question is certainly at present the central point of the Soviet Government's worries, and the negative reply which it is led to give to that question—*not without good grounds, too*" (my italics) "—is sufficient to explain the mood of the press."

And Sumner Welles, Assistant Secretary of State of the U.S.A., who came on a tour of Europe in 1940? "It should never be forgotten," he wrote, "that the Soviet Union did not desert the League. It was the great Powers which dominated the League in its later years that deserted the Soviet Union." Hitler in 1938, said Welles, counted "on the unwillingness of both France and Great Britain to align themselves with the Soviet Union in a war in Central Europe. Nor did he underestimate the influence of those in the two western countries who still believed that German domination of Europe was preferable to the growth of Russian power."

Here is another contemporary voice, that of Professor A. B. Keith—though a Tory professor of constitutional history, and not a diplomat, yet for many years a close student of modern diplomacy—writing on the very day of Munich (the note is reproduced in his book of 1940, *The Causes of the War*). Chamberlain and Daladier, he said, had "acquired the rank of peacemakers by the convenient method of imposing further surrenders on Czechoslovakia." They knew that Mussolini and Hitler were demanding wholesale concessions to the demands of Hungary and Poland. With German armies in possession of the ceded areas of Czechoslovakia, the latter—and Chamberlain and Daladier as well—would be compelled once more to accept the dictation of Germany and Italy. "The way will be made ready for the undisputed control by these Powers of eastern Europe, preparatory to advance against Russia."

Some of the statements quoted are clear and unambiguous, others couched in diplomatic language. But their principal meaning cannot be misunderstood.

Let us turn to later writers, historians. Three will suffice: none of them can be accused of being pro-Communist.

Professor L. B. Namier wrote in 1948: "Munich was a Four-Power Pact dictated by the Axis. Could the Western Powers believe that Hitler had reached the limit of his ambitions (and would now re-start painting Christmas cards), or were they willing to remain passive spectators if, for instance, he turned against the U.S.S.R.?" To ask a question in such a way is to answer it. Referring to Hitler's "offer" to Poland on October 24, 1938—to give up Danzig, allow a German corridor across the Polish Corridor, and sign an alliance with Germany—Namier wrote: "It had been assumed in the West that such an understanding would be directed against Russia, and aim at conquering *Lebensraum* in the East for both partners." And later on he added: "Ramsay MacDonald's 'Four-Power Pact' of 1933, associating the Western Powers with the Dictators, delineated the pattern of policy which led to the Munich surrender. . . . Did they mean to deflect Hitler against the East, especially against the Soviet Union? They yearned for peace all round; but if there had to be aggression, they like everyone else hoped that Hitler would start on some country other than their own, and at as great a distance from it as possible." The difference between this policy and that of the U.S.S.R., on which Professor Namier did not enlarge, was that the latter strove, not to "deflect" Hitler westwards, but to enlist the help of Britain and France in checkmating him.

Then there is the *Survey of International Affairs* of Chatham House for 1938—a volume published in 1951, far less unkind to Chamberlain than Sir Lewis Namier, and one which strains every nerve to find something soothing to say about him. Writing of the British Conservatives who were in power, it says "a very numerous element" (to avoid saying "the overwhelming majority") were "peculiarly receptive of the German propaganda harping constantly on the theme that Britain had no interests in Central Europe, while the Reich had no intention of interfering with British interests in other continents." In France, "for the bulk of the bourgeoisie, Bolshevism was the enemy": and the "Right" (to avoid saying *all* the bourgeois parties, since the Government included both Radicals and Socialists, but none of the Right) "believed that Nazism could be canalised, that its anti-Bolshevism was a real matter of faith, that the peace of Western civilisation could be saved by deflecting Germany to the conquest of the East."

Lastly we have the historian of the League of Nations—a non-party international civil servant for many years, correct and obviously anxious to be objective. From its exclusion from the negotiations over Czechoslovakia, writes Mr. Walters, and from the failure of its efforts to revive the security system of the Covenant (efforts which Britain took the lead in opposing), "the Soviet Government was justified in concluding that the British and French did not desire its participation in their search for peace. It drew also, doubtless with less justification, the conclusion that they secretly hoped to see Russia attacked by Germany and that, if this should happen, she could not count upon their help." The only comment which the reader will probably make, after all the foregoing, will be to ask: why with "less justification"?

There can be no reasonable doubt that we have the answer to the question asked in the title of this . . . [section]. The British and French Governments acted as they did in 1938 because they hoped, by handing over Czechoslovakia to Hitler, to keep the door open for him to commit further aggression in the east of Europe, preferably against the U.S.S.R. This was no new idea for the British Government: it had been an integral strand in their foreign policy for many years, and particularly since 1933. For the French Government it dated from a little later, but not very much later. That this put them in danger themselves they did not believe: they were too sure of Hitler as their partner in this scheme, and perhaps they thought he shared their belief in the nonsense which the British Embassy in Moscow (and some others) were feeding to them, about internal conditions in the U.S.S.R. It seemed a winning card. All

that was now necessary, to back it up, was to build up their armaments as fast as possible, in order to make sure that Hitler kept his side of the bargain. Who would fail to choose attacking the Soviet Union—chaotic, militarily feeble, economically disorganised, politically oppressed, etc., etc.—rather than attacking powerful, democratic, prosperous and well-armed Britain and France?

That was the gamble of Munich: and there lies the error of calling it "appeasement." It was a good deal more than that.

If two gangsters, with an already long list of murders on their record, announce their intention of doing away with another victim: and two others, outwardly respectable businessmen, but who have been privately financing them for years in order to keep the gangsters away from their own well-lined safes, make all the arrangements with them for the new crime, each of the four may have his own little calculations. The calculations may be very different. The first two may be secretly planning to attack the second two, next time. The second two may be hoping that the next "job" they finance will rid them of a powerful business competitor—and of a pair of dangerous partners into the bargain. But for the moment these diverging motives are secondary. For the time being all four are partners—partners in a conspiracy, with both immediate and long-term ends. The latter may differ: the short-term ends coincide.

That is what went on in 1938, and culminated at Munich. For the moment, the victim was Czechoslovakia. For Hitler, seconded by his Italian partner, it was one more of his chain of "improvisations" on the road to fulfilment of *Mein Kampf*. For the British and French Governments, it was one more inducement to Hitler to go East—of course observing their interests—and ultimately to attack the Soviet Union. Which of these hopes would be realised, only the future could tell. But for the moment the conspiracy was certain—and all four were partners in it, their several parts in it determined by their circumstances.

Munich was a conspiracy for aggression.

Keith Eubank

THE RIDDLE OF MUNICH

Going over much the same ground as others, Keith Eubank adds a dimension to the usual description of the military unpreparedness of France and Britain. In his opinion not only were the forces of these powers insufficient to meet Hitler's, but equally important was the lack of both strategic plans and the will to fight. Eubank is an American historian who has also published *Paul Cambon: Master Diplomatist* (1960), and is presently Professor of History at Queens College of the City University of New York. His restatement of the reasons why Munich was a tragic necessity, when compared with the views of Shirer and Wheeler-Bennett, raises the question of the causes of this lack of will. Was it that the leaders of Britain and France failed in their leadership?

IN the story of the Munich Agreement there is a riddle. Was it only surrender to Hitler's bluff? If Britain and France had stood fast, resolute in their determination to resist, would Czechoslovak independence and world peace have been saved? Or was the Agreement unavoidable under the circumstances? Was it a "tragic necessity"?

To denounce the Munich Agreement as cowardly surrender is simple, but there is more to the tale. Other forces sent Chamberlain and Daladier to Munich. They did not go there out of sheer folly. They made the journey because it seemed the only alternative to a war no one wanted.

In 1938 the Munich Agreement seemed sensible to many who fancied themselves sane, sober, and Christian. It was far better than another world war. Because the Sudetens wanted to become a part of Germany, they seemed a poor excuse for bloodshed. The Treaty of Versailles was wicked; another world war was unthinkable. If appeasing Hitler with the Sudetenland avoided a world war, peace was preferred. There seemed to be no way to prevent German armies from overrunning Czechoslovakia.

There was an attempt to scientifically sample public opinion during the September crisis. This sampling revealed that 70 per cent of those contacted in one London borough reacted favorably to Chamberlain's flight to visit Hitler on September 15. At the time of the Godesberg meeting, the opposition to Chamberlain had risen to 40 per cent, according to a similar sampling; but the opposition dropped on September 30 to 10 per cent, with 54 per cent favoring him and 26 per cent expressing no opinion. After September 30, however, the chorus of approval seemed proof of public assent, regardless of the wisdom of the Agreement. Every sign in France and Great Britain indicated the satisfaction of the man in the street with the Munich Agreement. The few dissenters were drowned out by those who wanted peace and had no wish to die for Czechoslovakia. To the politicians the Munich Agreement seemed justified by public opinion.

Of these politicians, none has been more condemned for the Munich Agreement than Chamberlain. He did not accept the Munich Agreement out of cowardice but because he was unwilling to drag the nation into a world war over an issue that did not seem worth the loss of countless lives. He doubted that the nation would have followed him into a war to coerce a minority who wanted to exercise the right of self-determination. He preferred to seek a formula satisfying Hitler's political demands and then to solve the Anglo-German economic problems because these were to him the most important.

To the end of his life, Chamberlain believed that his policy had been the only one possible in 1938, given the spirit of the time and the hostility of the Opposition. But the excuse of a strong Opposition meant little within the House of Commons where the Tories had a safe majority.

Chamberlain was strengthened in his resolution to appease Hitler by the pathetic condition of the French government and the Premier. Although Daladier accurately evaluated Hitler's aggression, he would not lead his nation into a war over Czechoslovakia. He blamed everyone else for the sins of France: British lack of armaments, Britain's refusal to support France, Polish hostility towards Czechoslovakia, Russian legalism over the alliance, and United States' isolationism. It was sheer folly, he told the National Assembly in 1946, to fight Germany alone: France could be engaged to fight Germany only within a coalition.

In 1938, France was alone except for the help provided by the British fleet. There was no mighty coalition. There had been hopes that, if war with Germany ever came, Poland, Russia and Czechoslovakia would attack Germany from the east while the French armies remained behind the Maginot Line; but in 1938, Poland was hostile and Russia preferred to watch rather than act. To save Czechoslovakia, France would be forced to mount an attack.

When the French government had concluded the 1935 alliance with Czechoslovakia, no one considered that France would ever be called upon to fulfill her obligations by attacking Germany. The alliance would provide a Czech attack on Germany, not a French one. Appalled at the bloody prospect of assaulting Germany in 1938, French politicians and generals deserted Czechoslovakia, using the Munich Agreement. The generals tried to excuse their desertion by launching a campaign to expose the inferiority of the Czech armed forces.

If France had ever seriously intended to aid Czechoslovakia, she would have made plans for an invasion of Germany. Such plans never existed, and without an invasion of Germany to draw off Hitler's armies, the Czech forces were doomed. No plans for an attack on Germany existed in 1938, because French strategy was defensive. The war of 1914–18 seemed to have proven the superiority of the defense over the offense. As a symbol of this philosophy, the Maginot Line had been constructed to withstand the expected German offensive.

Behind the Line the armies of France would be secure; casualties would be slight while French guns decimated the enemy. The Line made defensive strategy imperative; it nullified the Czech alliance; it confounded all hopes of a French offensive against Germany. If the French armies stayed on the defensive, however, the Czech armies would be left alone to face the German attack. The armies of France would become involved in the war only if Germany attacked the Maginot Line, but Hitler planned to attack only in the east.

There had not even been any planning with the Czech general staff. When General Ludvík Krejčí, the Czechoslovak chief of staff, proposed to Gamelin on June 18, 1938, that joint studies be made to insure unity of decision, Gamelin referred the question to his government. No action was ever taken because the French High Command had no intention of any offensive action to draw German troops away from the Czechoslovak frontiers. They followed the teachings of Marshal Henri Pétain, who believed that defensive strategy reinforced by the Line made alliances unnecessary.

There had not been any joint planning with the British general staff. Whatever plans the French may have had in September, 1938, were not passed on to the British, who only knew that French plans were based on defense rather than offense and that they would not leave the Maginot Line.

The failure of the staffs to confer was

also a result of policy of the British chiefs of staff, who feared that talks with the French would anger the Germans when Chamberlain was seeking appeasement and would involve the British forces in commitments they could not fulfill. For similar reasons, cabinet instructions forbade any discussions of strategic plans with French generals. Until March, 1939, neither general staff had any definite idea of the strategic planning of the other.

Any plan to aid Czechoslovakia required a massive striking force—heavy tank divisions, possessing powerful engines, and long-range artillery with armor-piercing shells—poised on the western frontiers of Germany prepared to thrust deep into the vitals of the Nazi empire and draw off the German forces fighting in Bohemia and Moravia. Such an offensive force did not exist in 1938, mainly because of the attitudes of certain French generals and Daladier. In September, 1938, the French army had two light, armored divisions capable only of limited reconnaissance and protection for the infantry from other infantry but not from tanks. With heavy armored divisions and a resolve to attack, French forces would have broken through Germany and saved Czechoslovakia. Without these forces, Czechoslovakia was doomed.

Given the help of thirty to forty Czech divisions in 1938, France was stronger than Germany, but this strength was useless without an offensive strategy and plans for an invasion of Germany. Had war come in 1938, the French armies would have remained along the Maginot Line, facing only eleven German divisions, while the bulk of Hitler's forces slaughtered the Czechs.

The French air force would have provided little help in a war. It was antiquated, weak, and crippled by defensive strategy. In September, 1938, France had only seven hundred planes, and none was modern. The *Luftwaffe* had over twenty-eight hundred planes, and more than one thousand of these were bombers.

France lacked the industrial facilities necessary to sustain her air force in a modern world war. Between 1936 and 1938, the French government had ordered 761 planes, a month's production in Germany in 1938, and by September 1938, only 83 had been delivered.

The faith of the French in their air force was not improved by the reports of so eminent an authority as Colonel Charles Lindbergh. Appearing in Paris and London amid the September crisis, he preached peace at any price because the *Luftwaffe* was the strongest air force in the world and would "flatten out cities like London, Paris, and Prague."

The condition of the French air force was one more excuse that Daladier used to evade responsibilities which could have brought war. Another excuse was the condition of the British armed forces. Of these, only the Royal Navy approached a state of combat readiness when mobilized in 1938. However, there was no way for the fleet to aid Czechoslovakia because the sea coasts of Bohemia existed only in Shakespeare's mind.

The British army could offer no more than two divisions for service on the Continent, and Chamberlain was loath to promise even this. In 1938 only five, fully equipped, regular army divisions had been planned. They were to be trained for fighting a colonial war. Such a force would be unfit for offensive warfare against Germany. Noticeably lacking was any large force of mechanized armor, sufficient to pierce the German defenses and race to the aid of the Czechoslovak armies.

As late as November, 1938, the Chancellor of the Exchequer forbade the increase of the army to six divisions, using the argument of economy. One chief of staff observed that the Chancellor "was primarily concerned to insure that we had enough money left to pay the indemnity after losing the war."

After the occupation of Prague, the British army undertook to prepare thirty-two divisions—a force comparable in size to the Czechoslovak army which had been surrendered to Hitler without a fight. If Hitler had been faced in 1938 with thirty-two British divisions, thirty-five Czech divisions, and over one hundred French divisions, prepared to drive through Germany with all their strength, protected by a mighty air armada, there would not have been a Munich Agreement.

Of the three British military services, the status of the Royal Air Force had the most decisive influence on British policy in the September crisis. The R.A.F. did not measure up to the needs of the time either in defense or offense. In 1938 the R.A.F. could fight a German air force that had existed in 1936. The *Anschluss* forced the cabinet to approve a first line expansion to twelve thousand planes, to be ready within two years. This planned increase was known as *Schedule L;* only 10 per cent of the plan had been completed by the September crisis. This plan was consistent with the practice of expanding first line aircraft without creating the reserves, administration, and auxiliary services necessary to withstand a long conflict.

In September, 1938, less than 30 fighter squadrons were ready for duty. Only 5 of these were equipped with modern Hurricane fighters and none with Spitfires. In all there were 759 fighters, and the majority were outdated and so slow that German bombers could evade them easily. Although 93 Hurricanes were available, they were unable to fight above fifteen thousand feet even in summer because the guns could not be heated. Pilots for these squadrons were in short supply. The administration, reserve planes, and auxiliary services were lacking for a long war. The situation was similar in the bombing squadrons—insufficiency in modern planes, personnel, airfields, and servicing facilities. The R.A.F. was unfit for a world war.

Other means for air defense were lacking. Only 126 antiaircraft guns were available for the defense of London in September, 1938, and only 334 for the whole of the British Isles. The radar chain was incomplete, and the personnel were untrained in its use. Except for hastily dug trenches in parks, sufficient air raid shelters were lacking. Estimates of the probable number of killed and wounded that might result among the civilian population from air raids appalled the British government. Within

sixty days of the first air assault, 600,000 dead were expected, creating an additional problem in the disposal of so many bodies. To build sufficient coffins would have required over twenty million square feet of timber. Hospitals would have been clogged with over 1,200,000 wounded. Psychiatrists anticipated three to four million mental casualties within six months of the outbreak of war. There were no plans whatsoever to feed the population during the air attacks.

The inability of the British armed forces to wage modern war against Germany was known only too well within the government. When Chamberlain faced Hitler at Munich, the armaments and troops necessary to fight Germany did not exist, nor did the means to protect the civilian population. Thus it seemed wise to appease Hitler with the Sudetenland, for he could take all of Czechoslovakia if he desired while Britain could not stop him.

The riddle of the Munich Agreement is not solved by the testimony of the German generals, given after the war, that Germany was unprepared for a world war in September, 1938, and would not have fought had Britain and France resisted. Although Germany was unprepared for a world war in September, 1938, her armed forces were ready for a war against Czechoslovakia. Germany could not have held out against the Anglo-French forces in the west if they had been prepared to invade Germany, but emphasis on defensive strategy, lack of modern arms, and the Maginot Line made these forces ready to sit out the war.

At the Nuremberg trials, the German generals argued that their armies would have been delayed by the Czechoslovak fortifications, but if they had been willing to suffer losses they would probably have gotten through. Czechoslovak forces planned a withdrawal to avoid being outflanked on the old Austrian frontier where the fortifications were slight. Such strategy would have succeeded if the Anglo-French forces had been ready to sweep into Germany.

Now we know that the German armed forces were not as well prepared in 1938 as they were in 1939 or 1940, but they were ready for a war against Czechoslovakia—a limited war on one front. There was no need to worry about war on two fronts, because the British had little with which to fight, and the French had no intention of attacking Germany.

Now we realize that the intelligence estimates of the size of the *Luftwaffe* were exaggerated; however, in combat readiness, it far exceeded that of the Anglo-French air forces. Intelligence estimates were colored by the effects of the Douhet theory that bombers could score a swift, knockout blow. The Spanish Civil War increased the fears of total destruction from the air.

Although the *Luftwaffe* lacked heavy, long-range bombers to pound London and Paris, there were enough planes to overwhelm the Czech air force. Only a skeleton force would have been needed on the western front where there was no intention of attacking Germany. Hitler's forces could have defeated Czechoslovakia at will, aided by the Poles and Hungarians, if they cared to share in the loot.

If war had come in 1938, would the story have ended differently? If the Czechoslovak army had not been forced to divert too many troops against Poland and Hungary, probably the German armies would have been delayed a little longer in their conquest. Their ultimate victory, however, would have been certain, given time to wear down the Czech resistance and willingness to sustain casualties. Czechoslovakia would have received no direct aid from Britain and France and even less indirect aid than Poland received in 1939. While the Germans conquered Czechoslovakia, Anglo-French troops would have remained on the defensive within the Maginot Line.

If Hitler had then taken only the Sudetenland, without direct aggression against Britain and France, these governments would have been sorely tempted to make peace. This policy would have seemed logical and moral because Hitler was only taking what many believed had been torn from Germany by the Versailles Treaty.

If a general European war had come in 1938, the fall of France could have come a year earlier. The R.A.F. would not have been ready for the Battle of Britain if it had come in 1939, for *Schedule M,* the plan under which the fighters for the Battle of Britain were produced, was not drawn up until October, 1938, as a result of the Munich Agreement. It is doubtful if the Hurricanes and Spitfires could have been built in sufficient numbers to be ready for an earlier battle. Time was needed to bring *Schedule M* to completion. Time was needed to complete the radar chain which provided the eyes and ears of the R.A.F. in 1940. Had the Battle of Britain been fought in 1939, there is serious doubt that the R.A.F. could have withstood the *Luftwaffe.*

Arguments over the feasibility of war in 1938 prove little, however, because few in positions of responsibility in France and Britain wanted war over Czechoslovakia. Waging war would have meant that war had been accepted as the only alternative to a worse fate. In September, 1938, this did not seem to be the case either to the British and French peoples or to their governments.

If they would oppose Hitler, they must be resolved to go to the brink of war and beyond if necessary, but only Hitler was resolved to press on to war if such were necessary. Neither France nor Britain was resolved to stand fast against Hitler if war were the consequence. They were without the will and the means to resist. To those who prided themselves on their realism, there was no excuse for a world war and every excuse for appeasement.

When the four powers met at Munich, only Germany was prepared to pay the cost of victory—war. The governments of Britain and France wanted to avoid war over the Sudetens because such a cause was unworthy of the cost. Appeasement of Hitler through the Munich Agreement seemed worthwhile if it avoided a world war which Britain and France never wanted and for which they were unprepared in armaments and in spirit.

Here is the answer to the riddle of the Munich Agreement: to wage war required sufficient cause, a will to war, and the men and armaments. Because these were lacking in 1938, Chamberlain and Daladier had no other choice than to sign the Munich Agreement.

William L. Shirer

THE ROAD TO MUNICH

Both observer and historian of Nazi Germany, William L. Shirer published his first-hand account of German events in his *Berlin Diary* (1941), and almost twenty years later the results of his own experiences combined with exhaustive research in *The Rise and Fall of the Third Reich*. His journalistic career in Germany as correspondent for the Universal News Service, 1935–1937, and as representative of the Columbia Broadcasting Company in the following years enabled him to record history in the making. His study of the documents and memoirs published since the Second World War added depth and breadth to his own observations. In the excerpts below, he deals with the German plot against Hitler and with the troublesome questions of "bluff" and the risks of war in 1938. Does his analysis of these matters confirm or destroy the reasoning of the apologists for Munich? Does it convincingly refute the plea of necessity?

DEEP gloom hung over Berlin, Prague, London and Paris, as "Black Wednesday," September 28, dawned. War seemed inevitable.

"A Great War can hardly be avoided any longer," Jodl quoted Goering as saying that morning. "It may last seven years, and we will win it."

In London the digging of trenches, the evacuation of school children, the emptying of hospitals, continued. In Paris there was a scramble for the choked trains leaving the city, and the motor traffic out of the capital was jammed. There were similar scenes in western Germany. Jodl jotted in his diary that morning reports of German refugees fleeing from the border regions. At 2 P.M. Hitler's time limit for Czechoslovakia's acceptance of the Godesberg proposals would run out. There was no sign from Prague that they would be accepted. There were, however, certain other signs: great activity in the Wilhelmstrasse; a frantic coming and going of the French, British and Italian ambassadors. But of these the general public and indeed the German generals remained ignorant.

To some of the generals and to General Halder, Chief of the General Staff, above all, the time had come to carry out their plot to remove Hitler and save the Fatherland from plunging into a European war which they felt it was doomed to lose. All through September the conspirators, according to the later accounts of the survivors, had been busy working out their plans.

General Halder was in close touch with Colonel Oster and his chief at the Abwehr, Admiral Canaris, who tried to keep him abreast of Hitler's political moves and of foreign intelligence. The plotters, as we have seen, had warned London of Hitler's resolve to attack Czechoslovakia by the end of September and had begged the British government to make clear that Britain, along with France, would answer German aggression by armed force. For some months General von Witzleben, who commanded the Berlin Military District, and who would have to furnish most of the troops to carry out the coup, had been hesitant because he suspected that London and Paris had secretly given Hitler a free hand in the East and would there-

From William L. Shirer, *The Rise and Fall of the Third Reich* (New York, 1960), pp. 404–408, 411–414, 423–426. Copyright © 1959, 1960 by William L. Shirer. Reprinted by permission of Simon and Schuster, Inc., Publishers, and Martin Secker & Warburg Limited.

fore not go to war over Czechoslovakia —a view shared by several other generals and one which Hitler and Ribbentrop had encouraged. If this were true, the plot to depose Hitler, in the opinion of generals such as Witzleben and Halder, was senseless. For, at this stage of the Third Reich, they were concerned only with getting rid of the Fuehrer in order to avert a European war which Germany had no chance of winning. If there were really no risk of a big war, if Chamberlain were going to give Hitler what he wanted in Czechoslovakia without a war, then they saw no point in trying to carry out a revolt.

To assure the generals that Britain and France meant business, Colonel Oster and Gisevius arranged for General Halder and General von Witzleben to meet Schacht, who, besides having prestige with the military hierarchy as the man who financed German rearmament and who still was in the cabinet, was considered an expert on British affairs. Schacht assured them that the British would fight if Hitler resorted to arms against the Czechs.

The news that had reached Erich Kordt, one of the conspirators, in the German Foreign Office late on the night of September 13, that Chamberlain urgently proposed "to come over at once by air" to seek a peaceful solution of the Czech crisis, had caused consternation in the camp of the plotters. They had counted on Hitler's returning to Berlin from the Nuremberg Party Rally on the fourteenth and, according to Kordt, had planned to carry out the putsch on that day or the next. But the Fuehrer did not return to the capital. Instead, he went to Munich and on the fourteenth continued on to Berchtesgaden, where he awaited the visit of the British Prime Minister the next day.

There were double grounds for the feeling of utter frustration among the plotters. Their plans could be carried out only if Hitler were in Berlin, and they had been confident that, since the Nuremberg rally had only sharpened the Czech crisis, he would certainly return immediately to the capital. In the second

place, although some of the members of the conspiracy complacently assumed, as did the people of Britain, that Chamberlain was flying to Berchtesgaden to warn Hitler not to make the mistake that Wilhelm II had made in 1914 as to what Great Britain would do in the case of German aggression, Kordt knew better. He had seen the text of Chamberlain's urgent message explaining to Hitler that he wanted to see him "with a view to trying to find a peaceful solution." Furthermore, he had seen the telegram from his brother, Theodor Kordt, counselor of the German Embassy in London, that day, confiding that the Prime Minister was prepared to go a long way to meet Hitler's demands in the Sudetenland.

"The effect on our plans," says Kordt, "was bound to be disastrous. It would have been absurd to stage a putsch to overthrow Hitler at a moment when the British Prime Minister was coming to Germany to discuss with Hitler 'the peace of the world.'"

However, on the evening of September 15, according to Erich Kordt, Dr. Paul Schmidt, who was in on the conspiracy, and who, as we have seen, acted as sole interpreter—and sole witness—at the Hitler-Chamberlain talk, informed him "by prearranged code" that the Fuehrer was still determined to conquer the whole of Czechoslovakia and that he had put forward to Chamberlain impossible demands "in the hope that they would be refused." This intelligence revived the spirits of the conspirators. Kordt informed Colonel Oster of it the same evening and it was decided to go ahead with the plans as soon as Hitler returned to Berlin. "But first of all," Oster said, "we must get the bird back into his cage in Berlin."

The bird flew back to his "cage" from the Godesberg talks on the afternoon of September 24. On the morning of "Black Wednesday," the twenty-eighth, Hitler had been in Berlin for nearly four days. On the twenty-sixth he apparently had burned his bridges in his outburst at the Sportpalast. On the twenty-seventh he had sent Sir Horace Wilson back to London empty-handed, and the British government's reaction had been to mobilize the fleet and warn Prague to expect an immediate German attack. During the day he had also, as we have seen, ordered the "assault units" to take their combat positions on the Czech frontier and be ready for "action" on September 30—three days hence.

What were the conspirators waiting for? All the conditions they themselves had set had now been fulfilled. Hitler was in Berlin. He was determined to go to war. He had set the date for the attack on Czechoslovakia as September 30—two days away now. Either the putsch must be made at once, or it would be too late to overthrow the dictator and stop the war.

Kordt declares that during the day of September 27 the plotters set a definite date for action: September 29. Gisevius, in his testimony on the stand at Nuremberg and also in his book, claims that the generals—Halder and Witzleben—decided to act immediately on September 28 after they got a copy of Hitler's "defiant letter" with its "insulting demand" to Chamberlain of the night before.

Oster received a copy of this defiant letter [Gisevius says] late that night [September 27], and on the morning of September 28 I took the copy to Witzleben. Witzleben went to Halder with it. Now, at last, the Chief of the General Staff had his desired, unequivocal proof that Hitler was not bluffing, that he wanted war.

Tears of indignation ran down Halder's cheeks . . . Witzleben insisted that now it was time to take action. He persuaded Halder to go to see Brauchitsch. After a while Halder returned to say that he had good news: Brauchitsch was also outraged and would probably take part in the Putsch.

But either the text of the letter had been altered in the copying or the generals misunderstood it, for, as we have seen, it was so moderate in tone, so full of promises to "negotiate details with the Czechs" and to "give a formal guarantee for the remainder of Czechoslovakia," so conciliatory in suggesting to Chamberlain that he might continue his efforts, that the Prime Minister, after

reading it, had immediately telegraphed Hitler suggesting a Big-Power conference to settle the details and at the same time wired Mussolini asking his support for such a proposal.

Of this eleventh-hour effort at appeasement the generals apparently had no knowledge, but General von Brauchitsch, the Commander in Chief of the Army, may have had some inkling. According to Gisevius, Witzleben telephoned Brauchitsch from Halder's office, told him that all was ready and pleaded with him to lead the revolt himself. But the Army commander was noncommittal. He informed Halder and Witzleben that he would first have to go over to the Fuehrer's Chancellery to see for himself whether the generals had assessed the situation correctly. Gisevius says that Witzleben rushed back to his military headquarters.

"Gisevius," he declared excitedly, "the time has come!"

*   *   *

[After recounting the events of September 28th which led to the decision to hold the Munich conference, and noting briefly the reactions to the announcement, Shirer returns to the plot to overthrow Hitler.]

And what of the conspirators, the generals and the civilians, General Halder and General von Witzleben, Schacht and Gisevius and Kordt, and the rest, who shortly before noon on that fateful day had believed, as Witzleben said, that their time had come? The answer can be given briefly in their own words—spoken much later when all was over and they were anxious to prove to the world how opposed they had been to Hitler and his catastrophic follies which had brought Germany to utter ruin after a long and murderous war.

Neville Chamberlain, they all claimed, was the villain! By agreeing to come to Munich he had forced them at the very last minute to call off their plans to overthrow Hitler and the Nazi regime! . . .

In his interrogation at Nuremberg Halder explained to Captain Harris [attorney on the American staff at the Nuremberg trials] that there were three conditions for a successful "revolutionary action":

The first condition is a clear and resolute leadership. The second condition is the readiness of the masses of the people to follow the idea of the revolution. The third condition is the right choice of time. According to our views, the first condition of a clear resolute leadership was there. The second condition we thought fulfilled too, because . . . the German people did not want war. Therefore the nation was ready to consent to a revolutionary act for fear of war. The third condition—the right choice of time—was good because we had to expect within forty-eight hours the order for carrying out a military action. Therefore we were firmly convinced that we would be successful.

But now came Mr. Chamberlain and with one stroke the danger of war was avoided.

One can doubt that General Halder's first condition was ever fulfilled, as he claimed. For had there been "clear and resolute leadership" why should the generals have hesitated for four days? They had on tap the military force to easily sweep Hitler and his regime aside: Witzleben had a whole army corps—the IIIrd—in and around Berlin, Brockdorff-Ahlefeldt had a crack infantry division in nearby Potsdam, Hoefner had a panzer division to the south, and the two ranking police officers in the capital, Count von Helldorf and Count von der Schulenburg, had a large force of well-armed police to help out. All of these officers, according to the plotters themselves, were but waiting for the word from Halder to spring into action with overwhelming armed force. And the population of Berlin, scared to death that Hitler was about to bring on a war, would have—so far as this writer could, at first hand, judge them—spontaneously backed the coup.

Whether Halder and Witzleben would have *finally* acted had Chamberlain not agreed to come to Munich is a question that can never be answered with any degree of finality. Given the peculiar attitude of these generals at this time which made them concerned with overthrowing Hitler not in order to bring an end to

the tyranny and terror of his regime but merely to avert a lost war, it is possible that they might have acted had not the Munich Conference been arranged. The information necessary to establish how well the plot was hatched, how ready the armed forces were to march and how near Halder and Witzleben really came to giving the order to act has so far been lacking. We have only the statements of a handful of participants who after the war were anxious to prove their opposition to National Socialism, and what they have said and written in self-defense is often conflicting and confusing.

If, as the conspirators claim, their plans were on the point of being carried out, the announcement of Chamberlain's trip to Munich certainly cut the ground from underneath their feet. The generals could scarcely have arrested Hitler and tried him as a war criminal when it was obvious that he was about to achieve an important conquest without war.

What is certain among all these uncertainties—and here Dr. Schacht must be conceded his point—is that such a golden opportunity never again presented itself to the German opposition to dispose of Hitler, bring a swift end to the Third Reich and save Germany and the world from war. The Germans, if one may risk a generalization, have a weakness for blaming foreigners for their failures. The responsibility of Chamberlain and Halifax, of Daladier and Bonnet, for Munich and thus for all the disastrous consequences which ensued is overwhelming. But they may be pardoned to some extent for not taking very seriously the warnings of a "revolt" of a group of German generals and civilians most of whom had served Hitler with great ability up to this moment. They, or at least some of their advisers in London and Paris, may have recalled the bleak facts of recent German history: that the Army had helped put the former Austrian corporal into power, had been delighted at the opportunities he gave it to rearm, had apparently not objected to the destruction of individual freedom under National Socialism or done anything about the murder of its own General von Schleicher or the removal, on a dastardly frame-up, of its commanding officer, General von Fritsch; and—recently—had gone along with the rape of Austria, indeed had supplied the military force to carry it out. Whatever blame may be heaped on the archappeasers in London and Paris, and great it undoubtedly is, the fact remains that the German generals themselves, and their civilian coconspirators, failed at an opportune moment to act on their own.

Was the Franco-British surrender at Munich necessary? Was Adolf Hitler not bluffing?

The answer, paradoxically, to both questions, we now know, is No. All the generals close to Hitler who survived the war agree that had it not been for Munich Hitler would have attacked Czechoslovakia on October 1, 1938, and they presume that, whatever momentary hesitations there might have been in London, Paris and Moscow, in the end Britain, France and Russia would have been drawn into the war.

And—what is most important to this history at this point—the German generals agree unanimously that Germany would have lost the war, and in short order. The argument of the supporters of Chamberlain and Daladier—and they were in the great majority at the time—that Munich saved the West not only from war but from defeat in war and, incidentally, preserved London and Paris from being wiped out by the Luftwaffe's murderous bombing has been impressively refuted, so far as concern the last two points, by those in a position to know best: the German generals, and especially those generals who were closest to Hitler and who supported him from beginning to end the most fanatically.

The leading light among the latter was General Keitel, chief of OKW [High Command of Armed Forces], toady to Hitler and constantly at his side. When asked on the stand at the Nuremberg trial what the reaction of the German generals was to Munich he replied:

We were extraordinarily happy that it had not come to a military operation because . . . we had always been of the opinion that our means of attack against the frontier fortifications of Czechoslovakia were insufficient. From a purely military point of view we lacked the means for an attack which involved the piercing of the frontier fortifications.

It has always been assumed by Allied military experts that the German Army would have romped through Czechoslovakia. But to the testimony of Keitel that this would not have been the case must be added that of Field Marshal von Manstein, who became one of the most brilliant of the German field commanders. When he, in his turn, testified at Nuremberg (unlike Keitel and Jodl, he was not on trial for his life) on the German position at the time of Munich, he explained:

If a war had broken out, neither our western border nor our Polish frontier could really have been effectively defended by us, and there is no doubt whatsoever that had Czechoslovakia defended herself, we would have been held up by her fortifications, for we did not have the means to break through.

Jodl, the "brains" of OKW, put it this way when he took the stand in his own defense at Nuremberg:

It was out of the question, with five fighting divisions and seven reserve divisions in the western fortifications, which were nothing but a large construction site, to hold out against 100 French divisions. That was militarily impossible.

If, as these German generals concede, Hitler's army lacked the means of penetrating the Czech fortifications, and Germany, in the face of France's overwhelming strength in the west, was in a "militarily impossible" situation, and further, since, as we have seen, there was such grave dissension among the generals that the Chief of the Army General Staff was prepared to overthrow the Fuehrer in order to avert a hopeless war —why, then, did not the French and British general staffs know this? Or did they? And if they did, how could the heads of government of Britain and

France be forced at Munich into sacrificing so much of their nations' vital interests? In seeking answers to such questions we confront one of the mysteries of the Munich time which has not yet been cleared up. Even Churchill, concerned as he is with military affairs, scarcely touches on it in his massive memoirs.

It is inconceivable that the British and French general staffs and the two governments did not know of the opposition of the German Army General Staff to a European war. For, as already noted here, the conspirators in Berlin warned the British of this through at least four channels in August and September and, as we know, the matter came to the attention of Chamberlain himself. By early September Paris and London must have learned of the resignation of General Beck and of the obvious consequences to the German Army of the rebellion of its most eminent and gifted leader.

It was generally conceded in Berlin at this time that British and French military intelligence was fairly good. It is extremely difficult to believe that the military chiefs in London and Paris did not know of the obvious weaknesses of the German Army and Air Force and of their inability to fight a two-front war. What doubts could the Chief of Staff of the French Army, General Gamelin, have—despite his inbred caution, which was monumental—that with nearly one hundred divisions he could overwhelm the five regular and seven reserve German divisions in the west and sweep easily and swiftly deep into Germany?

On the whole, as he later recounted, Gamelin had few doubts. On September 12, the day on which Hitler was thundering his threats against Czechoslovakia at the closing session of the Nuremberg rally, the French generalissimo had assured Premier Daladier that if war came "the democratic nations would dictate the peace." He says he backed it up with a letter expressing the reasons for his optimism. On September 26, at the height of the Czech crisis following the Godesberg meeting, Gamelin, who had accompanied the French government leaders to London, repeated his assurances to Chamberlain and tried to substantiate them with an analysis of the military situation calculated to buck up not only the British Prime Minister but his own wavering Premier. In this attempt, apparently, he failed. Finally, just before Daladier flew to Munich, Gamelin outlined to him the limits of territorial concessions in the Sudetenland which could be made without endangering French security. The main Czech fortifications, as well as the rail trunk lines, certain strategic branch lines and the principal defense industries must not be given to Germany. Above all, he added, the Germans must not be permitted to cut off the Moravian Gap. Good advice, if Czechoslovakia was to be of any use to France in a war with Germany, but, as we have seen, Daladier was not the man to act on it.

A good deal was said at the time of Munich that one reason for Chamberlain's surrender was his fear that London would be obliterated by German bombing, and there is no doubt that the French were jittery at the awful prospect of their beautiful capital being destroyed from the air. But from what is now known of the Luftwaffe's strength at this moment, the Londoners and the Parisians, as well as the Prime Minister and the Premier, were unduly alarmed. The German Air Force, like the Army, was concentrated against Czechoslovakia and therefore, like the Army, was incapable of serious action in the West. Even if a few German bombers could have been spared to attack London and Paris it is highly doubtful that they would have reached their targets. Weak as the British and French fighter defenses were, the Germans could not have given their bombers fighter protection, if they had had the planes. Their fighter bases were too far away.

It has also been argued—most positively by Ambassadors François-Poncet and Henderson—that Munich gave the two Western democracies nearly a year to catch up with the Germans in rearmament. The facts belie such an argument. As Churchill, backed up by every serious Allied military historian, has written, "The year's breathing space said to be 'gained' by Munich left Britain and

France in a much worse position compared to Hitler's Germany than they had been at the Munich crisis." As we shall see, all the German military calculations a year later bear this out, and subsequent events, of course, remove any doubts whatsoever.

In retrospect, and with the knowledge we now have from the secret German documents and from the postwar testimony of the Germans themselves, the following summing up, which was impossible to make in the days of Munich, may be given:

Germany was in no position to go to war on October 1, 1938, against Czechoslovakia *and* France and Britain, not to mention Russia. Had she done so, she would have been quickly and easily defeated, and that would have been the end of Hitler and the Third Reich. If a European war had been averted at the last moment by the intercession of the German Army, Hitler might have been overthrown by Halder and Witzleben and their confederates carrying out their plan to arrest him as soon as he had given the final order for the attack on Czechoslovakia.

By publicly boasting that he would march into the Sudetenland by October 1 "in any case," Hitler had put himself far out on a limb. He was in the "untenable position" which General Beck had foreseen. Had he, after all his categorical threats and declarations, tried to crawl back from the limb on his own, he scarcely could have survived for long, dictatorships being what they are and his dictatorship, in particular, being what it was. It would have been extremely difficult, if not impossible, for him to have backed down, and had he tried to do so his loss of prestige in Europe, among his own people and, above all, with his generals would, most likely, have proved fatal.

Chamberlain's stubborn, fanatical insistence on giving Hitler what he wanted, his trips to Berchtesgaden and Godesberg and finally the fateful journey to Munich rescued Hitler from his limb and strengthened his position in Europe, in Germany, in the Army, beyond anything that could have been imagined a few weeks before. It also added immeasurably to the power of the Third Reich vis-à-vis the Western democracies and the Soviet Union.

III. THE SIGNIFICANCE OF MUNICH

Keith Eubank

THE MYTH

Keith Eubank in the last chapter of his *Munich,* from which we have already reprinted an excerpt, points out the misinterpretations of the Munich crisis in world diplomacy since 1938. He warns us against the misuse of the word "Munich" and at the end pithily summarizes what he considers to be the explanation of the Munich Agreement. After reading the views of contemporaries and historians, do you agree with Eubank, or do you find that he has included unimportant factors and omitted important considerations in drawing his conclusion?

THE Munich agreement soon became a myth, with truth distorted to serve new ends. Even before the Agreement had been liquidated in 1942, the West had begun creating the myth: had Russia been sincerely approached in 1938 by Britain and France, she would have eagerly rushed to the defense of Czech democracy, and Hitler's Reich would have been destroyed. Soviet Russia appeared to many as the only nation willing to fight Hitler and to defend Czechoslovakia, but Russia had never intended to do battle with Germany.

Diplomatic relations between the Western powers and the Russians during the war were colored by the myth that Russia had turned to the pact of August 23, 1939, because of pique over the Munich Agreement. No one profited so much from the Munich Agreement as the Soviet Union: she could pose as an opponent of Nazi Germany without being called upon to fight because of the French conduct in the Czech crisis.

By the same means, the Czech Communists and their leader, Klement Gottwald, who had led the party in a deliberate campaign to destroy the very existence of the Czechoslovak state, could appear as Czech patriots, eager to save the nation. The myth covered a tale of treachery when Communist informers betrayed the Czechs to the Gestapo during the occupation.

For the Communists, "Munich Agreement" became a convenient peg on which to hang their anti-Western policy. The Western capitalists had betrayed Czechoslovakia to induce Hitler to turn eastward against the Soviet Union. The loss of Czech lives in the fighting during 1944 and 1945 was blamed on the West as another trick to sacrifice Czechs to the Germans.

When Czech democracy fell before the Communist onslaught in 1948, it must have seemed to many Czechs that once more the West had betrayed them. Although the myth was not the sole cause for the coup, the Communists exploited it, saying that the capitalist West had deserted the Czech people in 1938 while the glorious Soviet Union had stood ready for action. Bourgeois capitalists had left the Czechs to the mercies of the Nazis because they feared the masses.

On the twentieth anniversary of the Munich Agreement, the East German and Czech communist governments issued a statement to keep the myth alive. "The events following the signing of the Munich Agreement prove that Munich was an anti-Soviet plot . . . preparing aggression against the first Socialist state of the world."

Using the story of the Munich Agreement, it was easy for the Czech Communists to warn of West German rearmament and to point then to Russia as the only true friend. Reports in the Czech press of Sudeten agitation, propaganda,

From *Munich* by Keith Eubank, pp. 295–300. Copyright 1963 by the University of Oklahoma Press. Reprinted by permission of the publisher.

and meetings since 1945 have all contributed to bolster Communist rule in Czechoslovakia. Sudeten activity in West Germany has reminded the Czechs of Western connections with Munich. Among the leaders of the present Sudeten movement are Germans who were judges, generals, and officials in Czechoslovakia during the German occupation. Their names and activities are widely circulated in Czechoslovakia to remind the Czechs of the past and to make them willing to endure the present passively.

Each spring Sudeten refugees hold rallies at which ministers in the government of German Federal Republic extol the Sudetens' right to self-determination and demand the linking of Bohemia and Moravia to the future Germany. To some of the refugee leaders, the Munich pact still has international validity. Because these Sudeten groups have declared themselves as opposed to Communism, they have received fervent support from American congressmen.

The myth of Munich became a potent force in American politics during the Korean war: it was present in the debate over the seating of Red China in the United Nations, the argument over bombing China, the firing of General Douglas MacArthur, and the collapse of French power in Indo-China.

When the North Koreans attacked South Korea in 1950, President Harry Truman and his advisers considered the attack similar to Nazi aggression in 1938. Memories of attempts to appease Hitler intensified their belief in the folly of standing by and letting South Korea succumb. Failure to meet this aggression could lead to World War III, just as the appeasing of previous aggressors had done.

As the Korean War dragged on, charges of appeasement tended to smother all sane discussion of Far Eastern policy. Senator William F. Knowland declared that "appeasement was surrender on the installment plan." He equated lack of decisive and forceful action with appeasement: "Talk of seating the Reds in the UN is appeasement. Talk of establishing a neutral zone in Korea is appeasement. Waiting around for Mao Tse-tung to become Tito is appeasement."

The question of the prosecution of the Korean War and the bombing of Manchuria produced the argument that the failure to wage total war was appeasement. General MacArthur informed Congress that such appeasement only bred more war. Speaking for those now branded as "appeasers," General Omar N. Bradley, army chief of staff, declared that appeasement was giving something to an aggressor without making a struggle or paying a price. Because such was evidently not the case in Korea, Bradley did not think he was practicing appeasement. Freed of any restraint after his firing by Truman in 1951, MacArthur proceeded to speak wherever opportunity afforded about appeasement policy in high places reminiscent of that practiced at Munich by Chamberlain and Daladier.

The Geneva Conference in 1954 over the division of Indo-China evoked cries of "another Munich." The United States observer, former General Walter Bedell Smith, defended the conference with another definition of appeasement. "Munich's a damned poor term," he retorted. "At Munich things were given away when there was no fighting. This is a war!"

When President Dwight Eisenhower returned from the Geneva Summit Conference in July, 1955, he had to make the usual airport speech immediately upon arrival. Although the weather was rainy, Vice-President Richard M. Nixon forbade umbrellas lest the nation be reminded of Neville Chamberlain and the Munich Agreement. To quiet those ghosts, Eisenhower spoke in the rain without any covering.

The Munich myth was given fresh life by Nikita Khrushchev when he opened the Berlin question in November, 1958. He announced that the West had failed to stop Hitler in 1938 when the Soviet Union had been so willing to oppose the *Führer*. The Western governments, he declared, had "tolerated and encouraged the policy of blackmail and threats pursued by Hitler." In 1961, Khrushchev intensified the Berlin question by dividing the city and resorting to extensive testing of nuclear bombs. The charges of "another Munich" and "appeasement" again beclouded diplomacy. Some argued that

Khrushchev was pursuing a policy modeled after that of Hitler's in 1938 regarding Czechoslovakia, with the East Germans playing the role formerly assigned to the Sudetens. Khrushchev was seeking to undermine the West by negotiation and threats, just as Hitler had done in September, 1938. Proposals to negotiate the crisis were damned as "appeasement" and "a new Munich."

The meaning of appeasement has become a part of the Munich myth. Now appeasement means surrender to the foe without a fight. Such was never Chamberlain's intent, for he meant to remove by negotiation the possible causes of conflict. He assumed good intentions on the part of Hitler and a mutual desire for peace and prosperity.

"No appeasement" has come to mean inflexible position offering no compromise whatsoever, thus making negotiation impossible. The danger of the "no appeasement" policy grows from the mistaken interpretation of the Munich story. According to the myth of Munich, Chamberlain and Daladier simply surrendered; if they had stood fast, refusing to compromise, Hitler would have backed down because he was really bluffing. There would not have been any war. Those who accept this myth demand a belligerent pose, thinking it will suffice to scare off the aggressor. If the aggressor will not be frightened, the supporters of "no appeasement" must then face war or back down entirely. "No appeasement" has come to signify courage to go to the brink of war. It does not mean courage to go beyond the brink and wage war if necessary.

To cry "No appeasement!" has become a symbol of courage and strength. The "non-appeasers" insist they are going to the brink of war, but they do not expect to back up their tough words with action. By misreading the Munich story, they have become convinced that the aggressor is always bluffing: to call his bluff will stop his aggression. The non-appeaser takes up an inflexible position, leaving no room for maneuver, and declaring, in effect, it will be his way or war. But is he fully prepared to fight a war? If need be, will he shoot first? Has he the necessary means to protect the population? Is he not himself bluffing and pursuing a course as potentially dangerous as that he condemns Chamberlain for taking?

At Munich the Western powers believed they were unable to plunge into a war in order to find out if Hitler was bluffing. To avoid being caught in such a dilemma, Chamberlain took what seemed the more practical course.

To the non-appeaser it seems so easy to act the part of a gun fighter in a western cattle town encounter in the 1870's. He forgets that it was not only the fastest draw that won, but also the man who shot to kill. Each gun fighter had to accept the risk of being killed or else back down. The non-appeaser believes that merely by taking the gun fighter's pose he can ward off a fight. To actually go through with the fight is not his wish, because he is not prepared for it. Herein has the myth of the Munich Agreement become dangerous.

The Munich myth is a product of ignorance. The non-appeasers offer a glib, facile explanation for the Munich Agreement because they cannot see the entire story in all of its tragedy. It was more than surrender to bluff. It was the product of the revisionist historians and popular misconceptions about the Versailles Treaty. It was the result of minority problems inherited from the Austro-Hungarian Empire, with all the accompanying hatreds and bitterness. The Munich Agreement was aided by pacifists and frightened politicians who dared not face the threat of an unthinkable war now become thinkable. It was created out of military weakness, fear of offensive warfare, and poor strategic planning. It was the failure of Europe and the United States to unite in a mighty alliance to stop the Nazi threat. It was the product of the decline of Britain and France as world powers. It was the tragedy of men who ignored the future danger to enjoy the ease of the moment. It was a story of free men who were unprepared to wage war against the tyrant: this was the truth of the Munich Agreement.

SUGGESTIONS FOR ADDITIONAL READING

THERE is an extensive and growing bibliography on the Czechoslovak crisis and the Munich settlement. In these pages, however, only the more readily available books and articles are noted. For a fuller list of works, see Keith Eubank, *Munich* and, best of all, Francis L. Loewenheim, *Peace or Appeasement? Hitler, Chamberlain and the Munich Crisis* (Boston, 1965), which provides a descriptive and critical guide to the literature of the subject.

Among the books devoted to the crisis, Keith Eubank, *Munich;* Andrew Rothstein, *The Munich Conspiracy;* Henri Noguères, *Munich;* and J. W. Wheeler-Bennett, *Munich,* from all of which selections appear above, will repay reading completely for their differing assumptions and analyses. An early defense of Munich is contained in W. W. Hadley, *Munich: Before and After* (London, 1944). The lengthiest examination is that of the *Survey of International Affairs 1938*, Vol. II: *The Crisis over Czechoslovakia, January to September 1938*, by R. G. D. Laffan, revised by V. M. Toynbee and P. E. Baker with an introduction by Arnold J. Toynbee (London, New York, and Toronto, 1951). Donald N. Lammers, *Explaining Munich: the Search for Motive in British Policy* (Hoover Institution Studies, 16: Stanford University, 1966) analyzes the Marxist explanation as found in such books as Rothstein's, and attempts to come to grips with it. Geneviève Vallette and Jacques Bouillon, in *Munich 1938* (Paris, 1964), summarize the press with extensive excerpts and provide a chronology and useful guides to people and newspapers. Boris Celovsky, *Das Münchener Abkommen von 1938* (Stuttgart, 1958) is a painstaking study with a minimum of bias.

As yet there are only a few published French documents on the crisis. The *French Yellow Book* (New York, 1940) contains only five on the Munich Agreement and the immediate reactions to it, but when the *Documents diplomatiques français, 1932–1939*, 2nd series (1936–1939) reach 1938, many more may be expected to appear. On the other hand, both the German and the British documents are fairly voluminous. The United States and Great Britain brought out *Documents on German Foreign Policy, 1918–1945,* Series D (1937–1945), Vol. I, *From Neurath to Ribbentrop (September 1937–September 1938)*, and Vol. II, *Germany and Czechoslovakia*, in 1949. The Soviet Russian government had already published German documents which it had captured: *Documents and Materials Relating to the Eve of the Second World War*, Vol. I (November 1937–1938), and Vol. II, *The Dirksen Papers (1938–1939)* (New York, 1948), of which the latter, including reports of conversations with Chamberlain by the German ambassador, is the more valuable. The documentary evidence against German war criminals prepared by the American and British prosecuting staffs for the Nuremberg trials contains enlightening references to the Munich crisis: *Nazi Conspiracy and Aggression*, 8 Vols. (Washington, 1946–48). The third series of *Documents on British Foreign Policy, 1919–1939*, edited by E. L. Woodward and Rohan Butler, offers two volumes on 1938 (London, 1949), and constitutes the largest single collection of primary sources on the crisis. *New Documents on the History of Munich*, edited by V. F. Klochko *et al* (Prague, 1958) contains 61 documents from the Czech and Russian archives. The *Foreign Relations of the United States 1938*, Vol. I, *General* (Washington, 1955) devotes 256 pages to the "German-Czechoslovak Crisis." Finally, *Documents on International Affairs*, edited by Monica Curtis, 2 Vols. (London, New York, Toronto, 1942–1943) contains many speeches and other sources available at the time of Munich.

Excellent commentaries, mainly on the British and German documents, are: Gordon A. Craig, "High Tide of Appeasement: the Road to Munich, 1937–38," *Political Science Quarterly*, Vol. 65 (March 1950), pp. 20–37; Pierre Renouvin, "La politique anglaise pendant la crise de Munich," *Revue historique*, Vol. 205 (April 1951), pp. 260–272; and Bernadotte E. Schmitt, "Review Article: Munich," *Journal of Modern History*, Vol. 25 (June 1953), pp. 166–180. The tendentious character of the *New Documents*, published in Prague, is clearly brought out by F. Vnuk, "Munich and the Soviet Union," *Journal of Central European Affairs*, Vol. 21 (October 1961), pp. 285–304; and William V. Wallace, "New Documents on the History of Munich," *International Affairs*, Vol. 35 (1959), pp. 447–454. Wallace, who had been permitted entry into the Prague archives in 1956, not only criticizes the collection but adds some excerpts from Czech documents.

The memoirs or biographies of men connected in one way or another with the Munich crisis are numerous, but many of them, like the memoirs of Lord Halifax, throw little light on it. Among the British defenders of the Munich policy the most important are: Keith Feiling, *The Life of Neville Chamberlain* (London, 1946); Iain Macleod, *Neville Chamberlain* (London, 1961); James R. M. Butler, *Lord Lothian* (London, 1960)— a prominent Conservative appeaser; Nevile Henderson, *Failure of a Mission* (New York, 1940)—the British ambassador in Berlin; Sir Samuel Hoare, Viscount Templewood, *Nine Troubled Years* (London, 1954); John (Viscount) Simon, *Retrospect* (London, 1952); and Frederick H. (First Viscount) Maugham, *The Truth about the Munich Crisis* (London, 1944). British critics of Munich and the government's policy include: Leopold S. Amery, *My Political Life*, Vol. III, *The Unforgiving Years, 1929–1940* (London, 1955)—a prominent Conservative; Winston S. Churchill, *The Second World War*, Vol. I, *The Gathering Storm* (Boston, 1948); Alfred Duff Cooper (Viscount Norwich), *Old Men Forget* (London, 1953); Anthony Eden, *The Reckoning* (Boston, 1965); Hugh Dalton, *The Fateful Years* (London, 1957)—a Labour Party leader; Ian Colvin, *None so Blind* (New York, 1965; published in London as *Vansittart in Office*)—a study

of the backgrounds of World War II with the aid of Vansittart's papers.

Fewer French actors in the drama have published their memoirs and the most useful for the Munich crisis are those of members of the foreign service. Robert Coulondre, *De Staline à Hitler* (Paris, 1950), covers the years 1936–1939, when he was ambassador in Moscow (until October 1938) and in Berlin. André François-Poncet, *The Fateful Years: Memoirs of a French Ambassador in Berlin, 1931–1938* (New York, 1949), occupied a key position; while Léon Noël, *L'Agression allemande contre Pologne* (Paris, 1946), emphasizes the Polish attitude and reaction to the Czechoslovak crisis as he saw them from his post in Warsaw. Apart from the diplomatic corps, General Maurice G. Gamelin, *Servir: Vol. II, Le prologue du drame, 1930—août 1939* (Paris, 1946), gives his recollections as Army Chief of Staff; and Pierre-Etienne Flandin, *Politique française, 1919–1940* (Paris, 1947), a leading appeaser although not in the government in 1938, devotes a chapter to defending the Munich policy. A useful review of the memoirs of Bonnet, François-Poncet, Noël, Gamelin, and one or two others is that by Maurice Baumont, "French critics and apologists debate Munich," *Foreign Affairs*, Vol. 25 (July 1947), pp. 685–690.

The most valuable German memoirs are those of Herbert von Dirksen, *Moscow, Tokyo, London* (Norman, Oklahoma, 1952)—ambassador in London during the Munich crisis; Paul Schmidt, *Hitler's Interpreter* (New York, 1951)— official interpreter at Berchtesgaden, Godesberg, and Munich; and Ernst Freiherr von Weizsäcker, *Memoirs* (Chicago, 1951)—state secretary in the German foreign ministry. Testimony concerning the army plot against Hitler is given in Hans B. Gisevius, *To the Bitter End* (Boston, 1947); and Erich Kordt, *Wahn und Wirklichkeit* (Stuttgart, 1947), and *Nicht aus den Akten* (Stuttgart, 1950).

On the Czechoslovak side are *The Memoirs of Dr. Eduard Beneš* (London, 1954), and Hubert Ripka, *Munich: Before and After* (London, 1939). Ripka, who was close to Beneš, drew heavily upon the Czech embassy archives in London. Speaking from the Soviet Russian viewpoint is the former ambassador in London, Ivan Maisky, *Who Helped Hitler?* (London, 1964). Testimony from the sidelines, but much concerned with the crisis, are two Polish publications: Josef Beck (foreign minister), *Final Report* (New York, 1957), and Jean Szembach (under-secretary in the foreign ministry), *Journal, 1933–1939* (Paris, 1952); and one Italian, the Foreign Minister Galeazzo Ciano, *Hidden Diary, 1937–1938* (New York, 1953).

Sharp and penetrating criticisms of most of the documents and memoirs listed above are offered by L. B. Namier, *Europe in Decay: a Study in Disintegration, 1936–1940* (London, 1950). The prejudices of this well-known English scholar are well analyzed by D. C. Watt, "Sir Lewis Namier and Contemporary European History," *Cambridge Journal*, Vol. 7 (July 1954), pp. 579–600.

Lacking the benefit of "inside information" afforded by official documents published later, many contemporary publications by journalists and scholars have proved to be remarkably accurate. They are, moreover, valuable for their reflection of the knowledge and the temper of the times. A very good work on the background of the Czech-German conflict is that of Elizabeth Wiskemann, *Czechs and Germans* (London, New York, and Toronto, 1938; 2nd ed., 1967). For a brief but very readable and reliable exposition of the international context, as well as the Munich crisis, see Vera Micheles Dean, *Europe in Retreat* (New York, 1939). An unusually able galaxy of British and American journalists have published studies of value: The editor of *Foreign Affairs*, Hamilton Fish Armstrong, *When There is no Peace* (New York, 1939), an enlargement and extension of "Armistice at Munich," *Foreign Affairs*, Vol. 17 (January 1939), pp. 197ff.; the *New York Times* correspondent, George E. R. Gedye, *Betrayal in Central Europe* (New York, 1939; London, 1939, as *Fallen Bastions*); Joan and Jonathan Griffen, *Lost Liberty?* (New York, 1939); William L. Shirer, *Berlin Diary* (New York, 1941); the *Manchester Guardian* correspondent in Paris, Alexander Werth, *France and Munich: Before and After the Surrender* (New York, 1939). Highly critical of the Munich Agreement are the American political scientist Frederick L. Schuman, *Europe on the Eve, 1933–1939* (New York and London, 1939); and the British historian R. W. Seton-Watson, *Munich and the Dictators* (London, 1939), expanded in *From Munich to Danzig* (London, 1939). A group of American and English authorities deal with "The Passing of Czechoslovakia" in Robert J. Kerner, ed., *Czechoslovakia: twenty years of independence* (Berkeley and Los Angeles, 1940).

As much if not more attention has been paid by historians to appeasement, especially that of the British, as to the Munich Agreement itself. Margaret George, *The Warped Vision: British Foreign Policy, 1933–1939* (Pittsburgh, 1965), attempts to reach an understanding of the motives of the appeasers. In addition to Gilbert Martin's *Roots of Appeasement*, from which a selection appears above, he and Richard Gott, *The Appeasers* (Boston, 1963), examine the objectives before and after Munich. The *History of the Times*, Vol. IV (London, 1952), throws light upon the attitudes of the editors who constantly advocated agreement with Germany. William R. Rock, *Appeasement on Trial: British Foreign Policy and its Critics, 1938–1939* (London, 1966), concentrates upon the opponents of appeasement in order to discover what forces led Chamberlain to change his mind in March 1939. A most revealing and readable study is that of A. L. Rowse, *Appeasement: a Study in Political Decline, 1933–1939* (New York, 1961), who knew personally all the leading appeasers of the 'thirties and believes that the government pursued appeasement out of ignorance and wrongheadedness. Despite the views of many studies of appeasement, D. C. Watt, "Appeasement: the Rise of a Revisionist School?" *Political Quarterly*, Vol. 36 (1965), pp. 191–213, argues that the assumptions adopted before the publication of certain documents have not been revised and should be re-examined in the light of the primary source material.

On the crisis itself, however, there are still areas of disagreement that cannot be cleared up on the basis of present sources. One is Soviet Russian policy and especially its relation to Czechoslovakia. Light on the latter aspect is supplied by Beneš's wartime secretary, Edward Táborsky, "Beneš and the Soviets," *Foreign Affairs*, Vol. 27 (January 1949), pp. 302–314; and by the historian William V. Wallace, "The Foreign Policy of President Beneš in the Approach to Munich," *Slavonic and East European Review*, December 1960, pp. 108–136. Max Beloff devotes a chapter to Munich in his *Foreign Policy of Soviet Russia, 1929–1941*, Vol. II (London, 1949). Two recent studies throw light upon Czech-German relations and suggest possible reassessments of Beneš's policies: Wenzel Jaksch, *Europe's Road to Potsdam* (New York, 1963)—embodying reminiscences of a Sudeten German Socialist;

and Johann Wolfgang Bruegel, *Tschechen und Deutsche, 1918–1938* (Munich, 1967). On another moot subject, two studies dealing with the German army, throw light on the plot against Hitler: John W. Wheeler-Bennett, *The Nemesis of Power: the German Army in Politics, 1918–1945* (New York, 1954); and, especially valuable, Robert J. O'Neil, *The German Army and the Nazi Party, 1933–1939* (London, 1966).

Finally, on British policy, a judicious presentation of the pros and cons of Munich is that of the well-known English diplomatic historian Sir Charles Webster, "Munich Reconsidered: a Survey of British Policy," *International Affairs*, Vol. 37 (1961), pp. 137–153. A summation which offers some unusual insights into the weaknesses of Munich policy-making is presented by the equally well-known student of international relations, Pierre Renouvin, *Les Crises du XXᵉ Siècle (Histoire des Relations Internationales*, Vol. VIII, Part II, Paris, 1958).

880-5974
5-12

1 2 3 4 5 6 7 8 9 10